hamlyn cookery club

Noodles and stir-fries

hamlyn cookery club

Noodles and
stir-fries

First published in 2000 by Hamlyn
an imprint of Octopus Publishing Group Ltd
2–4 Heron Quays
London E14 4JP

British Library Cataloguing-in-Publication Data
A catalogue record for this book is available from the
British Library.

ISBN 0 600 60002 5

Printed in China

Copy Editor: Heather Thomas
Creative Director: Keith Martin
Design Manager: Bryan Dunn
Designer: Ginny Zeal
Jacket Photography: Sean Myers
Picture Researcher: Christine Junemann
Senior Production Controller: Katherine Hockley

Notes

1 Both metric and imperial measurements have been given in
all recipes. Use one set of measurements only and not a
mixture of both.

2 Standard level spoon measurements are used in all recipes.
1 tablespoon = one 15 ml spoon
1 teaspoon = one 5 ml spoon

3 Eggs should be medium unless otherwise stated. The
Department of Health advises that eggs should not be
consumed raw. This book may contain dishes made with
raw or lightly cooked eggs. It is prudent for more
vulnerable people such as pregnant or nursing mothers,
the elderly, babies and young children to avoid these
dishes. Once prepared, these dishes should be refrigerated
and eaten promptly.

4 Milk should be full fat unless otherwise stated.

5 Fresh herbs should be used unless otherwise stated.
If unavailable use dried herbs as an alternative but halve the
quantities stated.

6 Pepper should be freshly ground black pepper unless
otherwise stated.

7 Ovens should be preheated to the specified temperature
– if using a fan-assisted oven, follow the manufacturer's
instructions for adjusting the time and temperature.

8 Measurements for canned food have been given as a
standard metric equivalent.

Contents

Introduction

Stir-frying is an ancient form of Chinese cookery which is now popular in the West as well as in South-east Asia. It's quick, healthy, crisp and low in fat. The short cooking time – literally only minutes – helps to preserve the nutrients and the natural flavours of the food. The food is fried in the minimum of oil over a high heat, stirring constantly so that the ingredients are kept in constant motion. This ensures that the food cooks quickly and is sealed on the outside to hold in the natural moisture.

PREPARING INGREDIENTS

Although preparation can be a time-consuming business, it can usually be done in advance earlier in the day. Just store the prepared food in sealed containers in the refrigerator until you're ready to cook the meal. The ingredients are usually cut into strips or dice so that they cook rapidly and the maximum food surface is always in contact with the heat. The Chinese are very specific about how the ingredients are cut, chopped or sliced. Here are some general guidelines to help you:

- Cut all the ingredients to a similar size so that they cook evenly.
- Always cut meat across the grain to help tenderize it before slicing or shredding.
- Slice vegetables into matchstick strips or cubes, dice, shreds or slices. Slice diagonally if wished.

FOODS FOR STIR-FRYING

Virtually any food that can be cooked quickly can be stir-fried successfully. Choose from the following:

- **Meat:** use good lean cuts such as beef steak, pork tenderloin and lamb fillet.
- **Chicken and poultry:** shredded duck, chicken and turkey are all suitable. Check that the pieces cook right through to the centre.
- **Fish and shellfish:** white and oily fish, prawns, lobster, crab, scallops and most shellfish are great for stir-frying.
- **Vegetables:** choose from asparagus, aubergine, bamboo shoots, beans, bean sprouts, broad beans, broccoli, cabbage, carrots, celery, chillies, Chinese leaves, courgettes, fennel, greens, leeks, mangetout, mushrooms, onions, pak choi, peas, peppers, radicchio, rocket, shallots, spinach,

spring onions, sweetcorn, Swiss chard and tomatoes, plus many more unusual vegetables.

• **Nuts:** cashew nuts are often used in Chinese and Indonesian stir-fried dishes to add flavour and a crunchy texture.

FLAVOURINGS

Stir-fried food is usually tossed in a little oil – vegetable, groundnut or the more strongly flavoured sesame oil are the most commonly used. Soy sauce, nam pla (Thai fish sauce), oyster sauce, black or yellow bean sauces, hoisin sauce and sherry are all used to moisten and flavour the food. Fresh root ginger can be peeled and then thinly sliced, grated or shredded to add a distinctive aroma to a dish. Other flavourings include five-spice powder, chilli powder, spices and herbs, especially fresh coriander.

EQUIPMENT

• A wok is essential as it retains an intense, steady heat throughout the cooking process. With its round base and sloping sides, it is the perfect shape. The heat is spread more evenly over the entire surface as the food is stirred and tossed in continuous motion in the hot oil or sauce. After cooking, rinse the wok thoroughly in hot water and dry quickly to prevent rusting. Woks may be made of iron or steel. The iron ones are very inexpensive to buy, but if you don't have one, use a deep, heavy-based frying pan instead.

• Chinese cooks always use a cleaver for chopping meat, poultry and vegetables. If you feel nervous about using one of these, stick to your kitchen knives.

NOODLES

Whatever type of noodles you use, they always have to be soaked, boiled or steamed before stir-frying. Never overcook noodles until they are really soft and mushy – they should be slightly soft on the outside but still just firm inside. You can experiment with the following different types of noodles:

• **Egg noodles:** these are the most commonly used and can be bought in small packs in most supermarkets. They are usually cooked in plenty of boiling lightly salted water for 4–5 minutes, then drained.

• **Rice stick noodles:** these are made from rice flour and have to be soaked in warm water until they are soft before using as the recipe dictates.

• **Transparent (cellophane) noodles:** these transparent noodles are made from ground mung beans. Soak them in hot water for 5 minutes before using.

Vegetables

Spicy Vegetables

1.2 litres (2 pints) water
200 g (7 oz) transparent cellophane
   noodles
8 dried shiitake mushrooms
3 tablespoons sunflower oil
250 g (8 oz) Chinese cabbage or
   Chinese leaves, shredded
pinch of salt
1 large carrot, thinly sliced
125 g (4 oz) fresh spinach, cooked
   and chopped
Sauce:
1 tablespoon sesame seed oil
1 tablespoon soy sauce
2 teaspoons sugar
2 teaspoons sesame seeds
½ teaspoon salt

Put the water in a large saucepan
and then bring to the boil. Add the
cellophane noodles to the pan,
bring back to the boil and boil
rapidly for 3 minutes. Drain the
noodles well and set aside.

Put the dried shiitake mushrooms
in a bowl and cover with boiling
water. Leave them to soak for about
20 minutes and then drain the
mushrooms. Discard the hard stalks
and reserve the caps.

Heat 2 tablespoons of the oil in a
deep wok or frying pan and add the
Chinese cabbage or leaves and salt.
Stir-fry for 2 minutes and then
remove. Heat the remaining oil in

the wok or pan and then stir-fry the
carrot for 1 minute. Add the cooked
cabbage with the spinach and the
soaked mushrooms and stir-fry over
a high heat for 2 minutes.

Make the sauce by putting all the
ingredients in a small pan over a
moderate heat and stirring well.
Bring to the boil and then pour over
the vegetables in the wok. Add the
cellophane noodles and toss well
until thoroughly combined. Heat
through and serve immediately.

Serves 4

Baby Vegetable Stir-fry with Orange and Oyster Sauce

2 tablespoons olive or walnut oil
175 g (6 oz) carrots, cut into
   matchstick strips
175 g (6 oz) whole baby sweetcorn
175 g (6 oz) small button mushrooms
salt and pepper
parsley sprigs, to garnish
Sauce:
2 teaspoons cornflour
4 tablespoons water
finely grated rind and juice of 1 large
   orange
2 tablespoons oyster sauce
1 tablespoon dry sherry or sherry
   vinegar

Prepare the sauce by blending the
cornflour in a jug with the water.
Add the orange rind and juice,
oyster sauce and sherry or vinegar.
Stir well to combine.

Heat a wok until hot. Add the oil
and heat over a moderate heat until
hot but not smoking. Add the
carrots and baby sweetcorn and stir-
fry for 5 minutes, then add the
mushrooms and stir-fry briskly for
another 3–4 minutes.

Pour in the sauce mixture and
bring to the boil over a high heat,
stirring constantly until the sauce is
thickened and glossy. Add salt and
pepper to taste, garnish with parsley
and serve at once.

Serves 4–6

Oriental Vegetable Stir-fry

The combination of fresh vegetables and tofu (bean curd) makes this a nutritious vegetarian main course, especially if served with brown rice.

2 teaspoons cornflour

8 tablespoons water

3 tablespoons soy sauce

2 star anise

2 tablespoons groundnut or vegetable oil

1 small onion, thinly sliced

125 g (4 oz) green beans, cut into 4 cm (1½ inch) lengths

2 celery sticks, diagonally sliced

½ each red, yellow and green peppers, cored, deseeded and cut into 4 cm (1½ inch) strips

125 g (4 oz) piece mooli, peeled and cut into thin 4 cm (1½ inch) strips

2.5 cm (1 inch) piece of fresh root ginger, peeled and crushed

2 garlic cloves, crushed

300 g (10 oz) packet tofu, drained, dried and then cut into 4 cm (1½ inch) strips

Blend the cornflour in a jug with 2 tablespoons of the water, then add the remaining water, the soy sauce and star anise. Stir well to combine and set aside.

Heat a wok until hot. Add half of the oil and place over a moderate heat until hot. Add the onion and green beans and then stir-fry for 2 minutes. Add the celery and stir-fry for a further 2 minutes, then add the peppers and mooli and stir-fry for a further 2 minutes. Remove from the wok and set aside.

Heat the remaining oil in the wok, add the ginger and garlic and stir-fry over a gentle heat for 2–3 minutes to blend the flavours without browning the ingredients. Pour in the cornflour mixture and bring to the boil, stirring constantly until thickened and glossy. Discard the star anise. Return the vegetables to the wok, toss over a high heat, then add the tofu and stir-fry briskly for 2-3 minutes until heated through and evenly combined with the vegetables. Serve at once.

Serves 4

above: oriental vegetable stir-fry
right: ribbon vegetable stir-fry

10

Stir-fried Summer Vegetables

2 tablespoons oil

2 spring onions, sliced

2.5 cm (1 inch) piece of fresh root ginger, peeled and sliced

2 garlic cloves, sliced

2 chillies, deseeded and chopped

50 g (2 oz) button mushrooms

125 g (4 oz) baby carrots

125 g (4 oz) mangetout

125 g (4 oz) thin French beans

50 g (2 oz) bean sprouts

1 red pepper, cored, deseeded and sliced

few cauliflower florets

4 tablespoons light soy sauce

2 tablespoons dry sherry

1 teaspoon sesame seed oil

Heat the oil in a wok or deep frying pan, add the spring onions, ginger and garlic and stir-fry for about 30 seconds. Add the chillies and all the vegetables. Toss well and cook, stirring all the time, for 2 minutes. Stir in the soy sauce and sherry and cook for 2 minutes.

Sprinkle the sesame seed oil over the vegetable mixture, then pile into a warmed serving dish and serve immediately.

Serves 4–6

Ribbon Vegetable Stir-fry

Peeling whole vegetables into long 'ribbon' shapes is an attractive form of presentation. Any kind of vegetable peeler can be used, but, for speed, use a swivel-blade peeler.

2 tablespoons olive, walnut or vegetable oil

250 g (8 oz) carrots, peeled into ribbons

250 g (8 oz) courgettes, peeled into ribbons

1 green or yellow pepper, cored, deseeded and cut into thin matchsticks

2 garlic cloves, crushed

salt and pepper

Heat the wok until hot. Add the oil and heat over a moderate heat until hot but not smoking. Add all the vegetables and garlic and then stir-fry for 2 minutes. Add a little salt to taste and plenty of pepper. Pile onto plates and serve at once.

Serves 4

Chinese Vegetables

1 tablespoon oil
4 spring onions, chopped
250 g (8 oz) mangetout
250 g (8 oz) asparagus, cut into small pieces
125 g (4 oz) canned water chestnuts, drained and sliced
1 tablespoon light soy sauce
1–2 tablespoons dry sherry
½ teaspoon sugar
pinch of salt
1 teaspoon sesame oil

Heat the oil in a wok, then add the spring onions and stir-fry for 3 seconds. Add the mangetout, asparagus and water chestnuts, toss well in the oil and cook briskly, still stirring, for 1 minute.

Add all the remaining ingredients and continue stir-frying for about 3 minutes. Transfer to a warmed serving dish and serve immediately.

Serves 4

Stir-fried Mushrooms

50 g (2 oz) small Chinese dried mushrooms
1 tablespoon oil
1 teaspoon finely chopped fresh root ginger
2 spring onions, finely chopped
1 garlic clove, crushed
250 g (8 oz) button mushrooms
250 g (8 oz) can straw mushrooms, drained
1 teaspoon chilli bean sauce or chilli powder
2 teaspoons dry sherry
2 teaspoons dark soy sauce
1 tablespoon chicken stock
pinch of sugar
pinch of salt
1 teaspoon sesame oil
coriander leaves, to garnish

Soak the dried mushrooms in warm water for 15 minutes. Drain and squeeze dry, discarding the hard stalks.

Heat the oil in a wok, add the ginger, spring onions and garlic and stir-fry for 5 seconds. Stir in the dried and button mushrooms and cook, stirring, for 5 minutes. Stir in the remaining ingredients, mixing thoroughly to ensure that all the mushrooms are coated in the sauce. Continue to stir-fry for 5 minutes, until the mushrooms are cooked through and tender.

Transfer the mushroom mixture to a warmed serving dish, garnish with coriander leaves and serve immediately.

Serves 4

Tofu and Mushrooms

2 tablespoons oil

125 g (4 oz) lean pork, diced

4 spring onions, chopped

2 garlic cloves, sliced

1 green pepper, cored, deseeded and
diced

1 small cauliflower, broken into
florets

125 g (4 oz) small flat mushrooms

1 tablespoon dry sherry

3 tablespoons crushed yellow bean
sauce

4 cakes tofu, diced

Heat the oil in a wok or deep frying
pan. Add the pork, spring onions
and garlic and stir-fry for 2 minutes.
Add the green pepper, cauliflower
and mushrooms and stir-fry for 1
more minute.

Stir in the sherry and yellow bean
sauce and cook for 2 minutes. Stir
in the tofu and then cook for a
further minute. Spoon the stir-fried
mixture into a warmed serving dish
and serve immediately.

Serves 4–6

*left: Chinese vegetables; stir-fried
mushrooms*
right: tofu and mushrooms

Italian Broad Beans

Pancetta is the same cut of pork as bacon, except that it is cured in salt and spices and not smoked. It is available in many supermarkets as well as Italian food stores and delicatessens.

1.5 kg (3 lb) small young broad beans
    (unshelled weight)
2 tablespoons olive oil
2 tablespoons chopped spring onions
1 slice rolled pancetta, 1 cm
    (½ inch) thick, cut into 5 mm
    (¼ inch) strips
6 tablespoons chicken stock
salt and pepper
1 tablespoon chopped parsley, to
    garnish

Shell the broad beans and rinse in cold water. Heat the oil in a wok and stir-fry the spring onions for 30 seconds. Add the pancetta and stir well. Add the broad beans and salt and pepper, toss well in the oil and pour over the stock.

Cover the wok and simmer for 6–8 minutes until the beans are just tender. If there is any liquid left, remove the lid, increase the heat and boil rapidly, stirring constantly. Transfer the beans to a warmed serving dish, sprinkle with the parsley and serve immediately.

Serves 4

Asparagus and Mushrooms

500 g (1 lb) asparagus
50 g (2 oz) butter
1 slice rolled pancetta, 1 cm
    (½ inch) thick, cut into 5 mm
    (¼ inch) strips
250 g (8 oz) small button mushrooms
salt and pepper

Cut the asparagus into diagonal pieces, starting at the tip and then working down towards the stem end. Use as much of the stem as is tender and discard the rest.

Melt the butter in a wok, add the asparagus and toss well. Cook, stirring, for 2 minutes, without browning. Add the pancetta and mushrooms and cook for 5 minutes until the vegetables are tender.

Increase the heat and boil rapidly for 1 minute until all the liquid has evaporated. Season to taste with salt and pepper and serve immediately.

Serves 4

above: Italian broad beans; asparagus and mushrooms
right: *Burmese white cabbage and noodle curry*

Burmese White Cabbage and Noodle Curry

500 g (1 lb) white cabbage

3 tablespoons vegetable oil

2–4 garlic cloves, thinly sliced

1 teaspoon sesame seeds

1 teaspoon turmeric

1 tablespoon chopped coriander

6 spring onions, finely chopped

1–2 fresh green chillies, deseeded and finely chopped

1 red pepper, cored, deseeded and thinly sliced

200 g (7 oz) egg noodles

2 tablespoons fish sauce (nam pla) or puréed anchovies

shredded fresh coconut or desiccated coconut, to garnish

Shred the white cabbage in a food processor or slice it very finely by hand. Heat the oil in a wok or large frying pan. Stir-fry the garlic for 1 minute, and then add the sesame seeds and turmeric and stir-fry for 1 minute. Add the coriander, spring onions, chillies and red pepper and bring to simmering point.

Meanwhile, bring a large heavy saucepan of water to the boil and add the noodles. When the water comes back to simmering point, remove the pan from the heat and set aside to stand for 8 minutes.

Add the fish sauce or puréed anchovies and sliced cabbage to the wok or frying pan and cook briskly until the cabbage is tender but still retains some bite. Drain the noodles and add to the vegetable mixture. Serve hot, garnished with coconut.

Serves 4

Stir-fried Bamboo Shoots

6 Chinese dried mushrooms

2 tablespoons oil

2.5 cm (1 inch) piece of fresh root ginger, peeled and shredded

2 garlic cloves, sliced

6 spring onions, sliced

2 green chillies, deseeded and chopped

500 g (1 lb) can bamboo shoots, drained and sliced

2 tablespoons light soy sauce

2 tablespoons dry sherry

125 g (4 oz) cooked lean ham, shredded

Soak the mushrooms in warm water for 15 minutes. Squeeze dry, discard the hard stalks and slice the caps.

Heat the oil in a wok or a deep frying pan, then add the ginger, garlic, spring onions and chillies. Stir-fry for 1 minute over a high heat. Stir in the remaining ingredients, mixing well, and stir-fry for 3 minutes. Pile the bamboo shoots into a warmed serving dish and serve immediately.

Serves 4–6

Mushroom and Broccoli Stir-fry

2 tablespoons oil

175 g (6 oz) small broccoli florets

125 g (4 oz) whole baby sweetcorn

1 large leek, chopped

1 yellow pepper, cored, deseeded and
cubed

375 g (12 oz) closed cup mushrooms,
quartered

3 tablespoons light soy sauce

1 tablespoon clear honey

2 teaspoons ground ginger

425 g (14 oz) can cannellini beans,
drained

Heat the oil in a wok or large heavy-based frying pan. When hot, add the broccoli florets and whole baby sweetcorn and stir-fry for 2 minutes. Stir in the leek, yellow pepper and mushrooms and then stir-fry for a further 2 minutes.

Stir in the soy sauce, honey, ginger and cannellini beans. Cover the wok and cook over a medium heat for about 3 minutes, until the cannellini beans are thoroughly heated through. Serve immediately.

Serves 4

left: mushroom and broccoli stir-fry
right: Chinese carrot and mushroom stir-fry

16

Stir-fried Aubergines

2 tablespoons oil, plus extra oil
   (optional)
4 spring onions, sliced
4 garlic cloves, sliced
2.5 cm (1 inch) piece of fresh root
   ginger, peeled and shredded
2 large aubergines, cut into
   5 cm (2 inch) long strips
2 tablespoons soy sauce
2 tablespoons dry sherry
2 teaspoons chilli sauce
chopped red and green chillies, to
   garnish

Heat the oil in a wok or deep frying
pan. Add the spring onions, garlic
and ginger and stir-fry for about 30
seconds. Remove from the pan and
set aside. Increase the heat, add the
aubergine strips and stir-fry until
browned, adding more oil to the
wok as necessary. Remove from the
wok with a slotted spoon and drain
on kitchen paper.

   Pour off the oil from the wok.
Return the spring onions, garlic,
ginger and aubergine strips to the
wok. Pour over the soy sauce, sherry
and chilli sauce, stir well and cook
for 2 minutes. Spoon the aubergine
mixture into a warmed serving dish,
sprinkle with chopped chillies and
serve immediately.

Serves 4–6

Chinese Carrot and Mushroom Stir-fry

2 tablespoons sesame seed oil
175 g (6 oz) carrots, cut into
   strips
1 green pepper, cored, deseeded
   and cubed
250 g (8 oz) flat mushrooms, sliced
250 g (8 oz) can bamboo shoots,
   drained
2 tablespoons light soy sauce
2 tablespoons hoisin sauce
2 tablespoons vegetable stock

Heat the sesame seed oil in a wok or
a deep frying pan until hot. Add the
carrots and green pepper and then
stir-fry over a medium heat for 2–3
minutes. Add the sliced mushrooms
and bamboo shoots and stir-fry for
a further 1–2 minutes.

   Add the soy sauce, hoisin sauce
and stock and stir-fry for 1 minute.
Serve immediately while very hot.

Serves 4

Szechuan Aubergine

2 tablespoons groundnut or
  vegetable oil
1 x 375 g (12 oz) aubergine, cut
  lengthways into 5 mm (¼ inch) thick
  slices, each slice cut crossways into
  5 mm (¼ inch) strips
1 cm (½ inch) piece of fresh root
  ginger, peeled and cut into thin
  slivers
1 garlic clove, cut into thin slivers
1 green chilli, deseeded and finely
  chopped
2 spring onions, cut into 5 cm (2 inch)
  matchsticks
1 tablespoon cider vinegar
1 teaspoon sesame oil
Sauce:
2 tablespoons vegetable stock or
  water
1 tablespoon soy sauce
1 teaspoon yellow bean sauce
1 teaspoon sugar

Blend the sauce ingredients together
in a jug. Heat a wok until hot. Add
the groundnut or vegetable oil and,
when hot, add the aubergine strips
and stir-fry for 30–40 seconds.
Remove the aubergine with a
slotted spoon and then set aside.

Add the ginger, garlic and chilli,
stir-fry for a few seconds to blend
the flavours without browning the
ingredients, and then pour in the
sauce ingredients and bring to the
boil over a high heat, stirring
constantly until thickened.

Return the aubergine strips to the
wok and stir-fry for 2 minutes. Add
the spring onions and toss well to
combine. Sprinkle over the vinegar
and sesame oil and serve at once.

Serves 4

Stir-fried Spring Greens with Raisins and Pine Kernels

This dish can be made with fresh
spinach, which doesn't need blanching.

375 g (12 oz) spring greens
2 tablespoons walnut or olive oil
1 tablespoon butter
50 g (2 oz) pine kernels
125 g (4 oz) raisins
salt and pepper

Remove the stalks and any tough
ribs from the spring greens. Put
several leaves one on top of
another, and roll them up tightly
into a cigar shape. Cut crossways
into shreds, and then repeat with
the remaining leaves.

Bring a large saucepan of salted
water to the boil, and then add the
shredded spring greens. Bring the
water back to the boil and blanch
for 1 minute only. Drain the greens
immediately and then refresh them
under some cold running water.

Heat the wok until hot. Add the
oil and butter and place over a
moderate heat until foaming. Add
the pine kernels and raisins and stir-
fry for 2–3 minutes, then add the
spring greens and increase the heat
to high.

Stir-fry briskly for 2–3 minutes
until the spring greens are hot.
Season with salt and pepper to taste
and serve immediately.

Serves 4

Vegetable Chow Mein

250 g (8 oz) packet fine egg
  noodles
2 tablespoons sesame oil
2 carrots, peeled and cut into
  matchstick strips
1 green pepper, cored, deseeded
  and diced
3 celery sticks, diagonally sliced
250 g (8 oz) can water chestnuts,
  drained and thinly sliced
175 g (6 oz) Chinese leaves,
  shredded
175 g (6 oz) fresh spinach leaves,
  shredded
salt and pepper
Sauce:
2 teaspoons cornflour
4 tablespoons cold vegetable stock
 or water
2 tablespoons soy sauce
1 tablespoon dry sherry or sherry
  vinegar

Prepare the chow mein sauce. Blend the cornflour in a jug with 2 tablespoons of the stock or water, then add the remaining stock or water and the rest of the sauce ingredients. Stir well to combine.

Break the noodles up slightly and then cook in boiling salted water, according to the packet instructions. Meanwhile, place a wok over a medium heat, add the

sesame oil and heat until it is hot but not smoking.

Add the carrots, pepper, celery and water chestnuts and stir-fry for 2–3 minutes. Add the Chinese leaves and spinach and stir-fry for 1 minute. Pour in the sauce and bring to the boil over a high heat, stirring constantly until thickened and glossy. Remove from the heat.

Drain the noodles and add to the vegetables. Return the wok to a high heat and toss the ingredients together until evenly combined. Season to taste and serve at once.

Serves 4

above: Szechuan aubergine; stir-fried spring greens with raisins and pine kernels; vegetable chow mein

in the oil and have wilted. Add the soy sauce, sugar, salt and garlic and continue stir-frying for 3 minutes.

Pour off any excess liquid and then transfer to a warmed serving dish. Sprinkle the spinach with the sesame seeds to serve.

Serves 3–4

Stir-fried Ginger Broccoli

500 g (1 lb) broccoli
2 tablespoons oil
1 garlic clove, thinly sliced (optional)
2.5 cm (1 inch) piece of fresh root
   ginger, finely shredded
salt
½–1 teaspoon sesame oil

Separate the broccoli heads into small florets, and then peel and diagonally slice the stems. Blanch in boiling salted water for 30 seconds, drain well and then cool rapidly under cold running water. Drain thoroughly and pat dry.

Heat the oil in a large wok, add the garlic, if using, and ginger and stir-fry for 2–3 seconds. Add the blanched broccoli and stir-fry for 2 minutes. Sprinkle over the sesame oil and stir-fry for a further 30 seconds. Spoon into a warmed serving dish and serve immediately.

Serves 3–4

left: stir-fried garlic spinach
below: *stir-fried ginger broccoli*
right: *stir-fried spinach with tofu*

Stir-fried Garlic Spinach

1 kg (2 lb) spinach
2 tablespoons oil
4 spring onions, chopped
1 teaspoon light soy sauce
pinch of sugar
pinch of salt
2 garlic cloves, crushed
1 teaspoon toasted sesame seeds

Wash the spinach thoroughly and remove all the hard stems. Drain and pat dry with kitchen paper.

Heat the oil in a large wok or frying pan, add the spring onions and stir-fry for 30 seconds. Add the spinach and stir-fry for about 2 minutes, until the leaves are coated

Stir-fried Spinach with Tofu

375 g (12 oz) fresh spinach leaves
2 tablespoons groundnut or
 vegetable oil
½ x 300 g (10 oz) packet tofu, drained
 and cut into cubes
1 garlic clove, crushed
3–4 spring onions, diagonally sliced
2.5 cm (1 inch) piece of fresh root
 ginger, peeled and chopped
2 tablespoons soy sauce
½ teaspoon caster sugar

Remove the stalks and ribs from the spinach. Put several spinach leaves one on top of another, roll up tightly into a cigar shape and then cut crossways into shreds. Repeat with the remaining leaves.

Heat half the oil in a wok over a moderate heat until hot. Add the tofu and garlic and stir-fry for 2 minutes. Remove and drain on kitchen paper.

Wipe the wok clean with kitchen paper. Add the remaining oil and heat until hot, then add the spring onions and ginger. Stir-fry over a gentle heat for a few seconds.

Add the spinach, soy sauce and sugar and stir-fry for 1–2 minutes or until the spinach just begins to wilt, then return the tofu to the wok and stir-fry for a further 30 seconds to heat through. Serve at once.

Serves 4

Three-coloured Peppers

1 tablespoon groundnut or
 vegetable oil
2 celery sticks, cut into matchsticks
3 small peppers (1 red, 1 green,
 1 yellow), cored, deseeded and cut
 lengthways into matchsticks
2 courgettes, cut into matchsticks
50 g (2 oz) pecan nuts, finely
 chopped
Dressing:
2 tablespoons lime juice
1 tablespoon olive oil
1 tablespoon anise-flavoured liqueur
1 garlic clove, crushed
salt and pepper

Combine the dressing ingredients in a large bowl. Heat a wok until hot. Add the oil and then heat over a moderate heat until hot. Add the celery and stir-fry for 2 minutes, then add the peppers and stir-fry for 1 minute. Add the courgettes and stir-fry for 2–3 minutes.

Transfer the stir-fried vegetables to the bowl of dressing and toss well to mix. Cover and then chill in the refrigerator for 2 hours. Serve chilled, sprinkled with the chopped pecan nuts.

Serves 4

Dry-cooked Bamboo Shoots

2 tablespoons dried shrimps (optional)
2 tablespoons oil
500 g (1 lb) can bamboo shoots, drained
2.5 cm (1 inch) piece of fresh root ginger, peeled and finely chopped
50 g (2 oz) Szechuan pickled vegetables, chopped
2 teaspoons caster sugar
pinch of salt
150 ml (¼ pint) chicken stock
2 red peppers, cored, deseeded and sliced
1 tablespoon sesame seed oil

Soak the dried shrimps in some warm water for 15 minutes, if using, and then drain.

Heat the oil in a wok or a deep frying pan, add the bamboo shoots and stir-fry for 2 minutes until pale brown around the edges. Remove and drain on kitchen paper.

Add the ginger, shrimps (if using) and Szechuan pickles to the pan and cook for 1 minute. Stir in the sugar, salt and stock and then bring to the boil. Return the bamboo shoots to the wok. Add the red peppers, mixing well, and then stir-fry for 2 minutes.

Transfer to a warmed serving dish and sprinkle over the sesame seed oil. Serve immediately.

Serves 4–6

Tofu Fry

4 cakes tofu (bean curd)
4 tablespoons oil
1 garlic clove, sliced
2 small leeks, diagonally sliced
2 celery sticks, diagonally sliced
125 g (4 oz) button mushrooms, sliced
125 g (4 oz) lean pork, shredded
4 dried chillies
1 tablespoon chilli paste
1 tablespoon dry sherry

Cut each tofu cake into 3 thin slices, and then cut each slice into 2 triangles.

Heat half of the oil in a wok or a deep frying pan, add the garlic, leeks and celery and stir-fry quickly for 1 minute. Stir in the mushrooms and pork and stir-fry for 2 minutes. Remove from the wok and keep warm.

Heat the remaining oil in the wok, add the tofu and stir-fry for 2 minutes. Remove with a slotted spoon and then drain on kitchen paper.

Return the vegetables, pork and tofu to the pan, stir in the dried chillies, chilli paste and sherry and cook for 1 minute. Transfer the mixture to a warmed serving dish, discard the dried chillies and then serve immediately while very hot.

Serves 4–6

Chinese Cabbage and Mushrooms

8 dried Chinese mushrooms
500 g (1 lb) Chinese cabbage leaves
1 tablespoon oil
2.5 cm (1 inch) piece of fresh root ginger, peeled and shredded
1 garlic clove, sliced
3 chillies, deseeded and sliced
1 green pepper, cored, deseeded and sliced
1 tablespoon wine vinegar
1 tablespoon light soy sauce
1 teaspoon sesame seed oil

Soak the mushrooms in warm water for 15 minutes. Squeeze dry and remove the hard stalks. Tear the cabbage leaves into pieces.

Heat the oil in a wok or a deep frying pan, add the ginger, garlic and chillies and then stir-fry for 1 minute. Stir in the green pepper, soaked mushrooms and cabbage and cook for 1 minute. Add the vinegar and soy sauce and mix well.

Remove from the wok and pile into a warmed serving dish. Sprinkle over the sesame seed oil and serve immediately.

Serves 4–6

right: dry-cooked bamboo shoots; tofu fry; Chinese cabbage and mushrooms

Chicken and Poultry

Chicken with Walnuts

375 g (12 oz) boned, skinned chicken
   breasts
½ teaspoon salt
1 egg white
1 tablespoon cornflour, plus
   1 teaspoon
4 tablespoons vegetable oil
2 spring onions, cut into 1 cm (½ inch)
   lengths
2 slices fresh root ginger, peeled
3–4 dried red chillies, thinly sliced
50 g (2 oz) shelled walnuts, chopped
1 tablespoon yellow or black bean
   sauce
1 green pepper, cored, deseeded and
   cut into chunks
1 teaspoon sugar
2 tablespoons dry sherry

Cut the chicken flesh into small
cubes. Place them in a bowl with
the salt, and then mix in the egg
white. Finally, mix in 1 tablespoon
of the cornflour.

Heat the oil in a wok or a heavy
frying pan and, when it is hot, add
the chicken cubes. Stir-fry them
briskly for a few minutes until the
colour changes from pink to white.
Remove from the wok and set aside.

Add the spring onions, ginger,
chillies and walnuts to the hot oil in
the wok, then stir in the bean sauce.

Add the green pepper, return the
chicken to the wok and stir well.
Add the sugar and sherry, and stir-
fry for about 1 minute.

Mix the remaining teaspoon of
cornflour to a smooth paste with 1
tablespoon of cold water. Add to the
wok and blend well until thickened.
Serve immediately.

Serves 3–4

Shanghai Chicken

50 g (2 oz) egg noodles
2 tablespoons oil
5 cm (2 inch) piece of fresh root
   ginger, peeled and shredded
2–3 garlic cloves, sliced
500 g (1 lb) boned, skinned chicken
   breasts, very thinly sliced
1 carrot, cut into flowers
3 spring onions, finely sliced
2 celery sticks, thinly sliced
250 g (8 oz) can bamboo shoots,
   drained and sliced
1 green pepper, cored, deseeded and
   shredded
175 g (6 oz) bean sprouts
salt
4 spring onion flowers, to garnish
   (optional)
Glaze:
1 tablespoon cornflour
1 tablespoon soy sauce
6 tablespoons dry sherry
2 tablespoons stock
pinch of chilli powder

Put the noodles in a jug and cover
with boiling, salted water. Cover,
leave for at least 8 minutes and
drain. Mix together the ingredients
for the glaze, adding salt to taste.

Heat the oil in a wok, and stir-fry
the ginger and garlic for 1 minute.
Add the chicken, stir-fry for 1
minute, then add the carrot, spring
onions, celery, bamboo shoots and
pepper and stir-fry for 30 seconds.

Add the noodles with the bean
sprouts and stir-fry for 30 seconds.
Add the glaze, turn off the heat and
toss until the ingredients are well
coated. Garnish with spring onion
flowers, if liked (see page 72).

Serves 4

right: chicken with walnuts

Spicy Chicken and Peanuts

Adding peanuts or cashew nuts to a stir-fried dish gives it an interesting, crunchy texture. Make sure you use unsalted peanuts in this recipe or it will have an unpleasant over-salty flavour. If you enjoy really hot, spicy food, you might prefer to add a couple of deseeded chopped fresh green or red chillies to the wok with the spring onions and ginger. They will also add a lovely bright colour to the finished dish.

125 g (4 oz) unsalted peanuts

375 g (12 oz) boned, skinned chicken breasts

2 tablespoons oil

1 dried red chilli

2 tablespoons dry sherry

1 tablespoon dark soy sauce

pinch of sugar

1 garlic clove, crushed

2 spring onions, chopped

2.5 cm (1 inch) piece of fresh root ginger, peeled and finely chopped

1 teaspoon wine vinegar

2 teaspoons sesame oil

red chilli flowers, to garnish (optional)

Immerse the peanuts in a bowl of boiling water for about 2 minutes. Drain well, then remove the skins and place them on some kitchen paper to dry thoroughly. Cut the chicken into 2.5 cm (1 inch) cubes.

Heat the oil in a wok or a large, deep frying pan. When hot, crumble in the dried chilli, add the chicken and peanuts and stir-fry for 1 minute. Remove from the wok.

Add the sherry, soy sauce, sugar, garlic, spring onions, ginger and vinegar to the wok. Bring to the boil and then simmer for 30 seconds. Return the chicken, chilli and peanuts to the wok and then stir-fry for 2 minutes.

Sprinkle with the sesame oil and then pile the chicken and peanut mixture into a warmed serving dish. Garnish with red chilli flowers, if using, and serve immediately with some plain boiled rice.

Serves 4

left: spicy chicken and peanuts
right: cashew chicken

Diced Chicken with Chillies

Always handle fresh chillies with care when preparing them. Do not rub your eyes or mouth and wash your hands thoroughly afterwards. Better still, wear some rubber gloves.

2 tablespoons oil
1 garlic clove, sliced
375 g (12 oz) boned, skinned chicken breasts, diced
1 red pepper, cored, deseeded and diced
2 green chillies, deseeded and sliced
50 g (2 oz) bean sprouts
2 tablespoons soy sauce
2 tablespoons chilli sauce
coriander leaves, to garnish

Heat the oil in a wok or a deep frying pan, add the garlic and fry for 1 minute. Add the chicken and stir-fry for 1 minute. Stir in the red pepper and chillies and cook for a further minute. Stir in the bean sprouts, soy sauce and chilli sauce and stir-fry for 2 minutes.

Transfer the chicken and chilli mixture to a warmed serving dish, garnish with coriander leaves and serve immediately.

Serves 4

Cashew Chicken

375 g (12 oz) boned, skinned chicken breasts
1 egg white
4 tablespoons dry sherry
2 teaspoons cornflour
3 tablespoons oil
4 spring onions, chopped
2 garlic cloves, thinly sliced
2.5 cm (1 inch) piece of fresh root ginger, peeled and finely chopped
1 tablespoon light soy sauce
125 g (4 oz) unsalted cashew nuts

Cut the chicken into 1 cm (½ inch) cubes. Combine the egg white, half of the sherry and the cornflour. Add the chicken cubes and toss well until evenly coated.

Heat the oil in a wok, add the spring onions, garlic and ginger and stir-fry for 30 seconds. Add the chicken and cook for 2 minutes. Pour in the remaining sherry and the soy sauce and stir well. Add the cashew nuts and cook for a further 30 seconds. Serve immediately.

Serves 4

stir-fry for 1 minute. Add the chicken and marinade and cook for 2 minutes. Stir in the soy sauce, lemon juice and rind and chilli powder and then stir-fry for a further minute.

Pile the lemon chicken into a warmed serving dish, garnish with lemon slices and parsley sprigs and serve immediately.

Serves 4

Noodles with Chinese Chicken and Mushroom Sauce

8 Chinese dried mushrooms or 250 g (8 oz) fresh shiitake mushrooms
200 g (7 oz) boned, skinned chicken breasts, cut into matchstick strips
2 teaspoons cornflour
8 tablespoons soy sauce
4 tablespoons sherry
2 teaspoons salt
2 teaspoons sugar
325 g (11 oz) egg noodles
300 ml (½ pint) chicken stock
8 tablespoons vegetable oil
250 g (8 oz) bamboo shoots, cut into matchstick strips
250 g (8 oz) spinach, finely sliced
4 spring onions, finely chopped
2 slices fresh root ginger, finely chopped

Lemon Chicken

375 g (12 oz) boned, skinned chicken breasts
2 tablespoons dry sherry
4 spring onions, chopped
2.5 cm (1 inch) piece of fresh root ginger, peeled and finely chopped
2 tablespoons oil
1–2 garlic cloves, thinly sliced
2 celery sticks, diagonally sliced
1 small green pepper, cored, deseeded and sliced

2 tablespoons light soy sauce
juice of ½ lemon
shredded rind of 2 lemons
¼ teaspoon chilli powder
lemon slices and sprigs of parsley, to garnish

Cut the chicken into 7.5 cm (3 inch) strips. Combine the sherry, spring onions and ginger, add the chicken and toss well to coat, then set aside for 15 minutes.

Heat the oil in a wok, add the garlic, celery and green pepper and

Soak the Chinese dried mushrooms, if using, in warm water for about 20 minutes. Squeeze out the moisture and discard the hard stalks. Cut the mushrooms into thin shreds. Mix the chicken with the cornflour. Combine the soy sauce, sherry, salt and sugar in a bowl.

Bring a large saucepan of water to the boil, add the egg noodles and simmer for 5 minutes until soft but not sticky. Drain and place in a heated serving dish. Bring the stock to the boil and then pour over the cooked noodles.

Heat the oil in a wok and stir-fry the chicken, bamboo shoots, mushrooms, spinach, spring onions and ginger for 1 minute. Add the soy sauce mixture and stir-fry for 2 minutes. Toss with the noodles and stock and serve immediately.

Serves 4

Chicken and Leeks

½ **cucumber**
375 g (12 oz) **boned, skinned chicken breasts**
2 **tablespoons oil**
3 **leeks, diagonally sliced**
4 **garlic cloves, thinly sliced**
1 **tablespoon light soy sauce**
1 **tablespoon dry sherry**
1 **dried red chilli, crumbled**
1 **tablespoon chopped coriander**
salt
sprigs of coriander, to garnish

Peel the cucumber, cut in half and remove the seeds with a teaspoon. Cut the flesh into 2.5 cm (1 inch) cubes, place in a colander and sprinkle with salt. Set aside for 20 minutes, rinse and drain. Cut the chicken into 2.5 cm (1 inch) cubes.

Heat the oil in a wok, add the leeks and garlic and cook briskly for 30 seconds. Add the chicken and brown quickly for 1 minute. Add the soy sauce, sherry and chilli and stir-fry for 30 seconds. Stir in the cucumber and cook for 30 seconds. Transfer to a warmed serving dish and sprinkle with the coriander. Garnish with coriander sprigs and serve immediately.

Serves 4

far left: lemon chicken
left: chicken and leeks

Stir-fried Chicken Breasts

In this inspirational recipe, the chicken breasts are stir-fried, tossed in a piquant plum sauce and then served with light golden pancakes. If wished, the batter for the pancakes can be prepared in advance and set aside until you are ready to cook them and the chicken.

4 chicken breasts
2 tablespoons cornflour
2 tablespoons soya bean oil
1 teaspoon sesame seed oil (optional)
2 garlic cloves, finely chopped
250 g (8 oz) can sliced bamboo
　　shoots, drained
150 ml (¼ pint) Chinese plum sauce
Pancakes:
25 g (1 oz) plain flour
2 eggs, beaten
150 ml (¼ pint) water
1 teaspoon brandy
1 tablespoon sesame oil
pinch of salt
soya bean oil, for frying
To garnish:
4–8 spring onion fans
cucumber strips

Prepare the pancakes. Sift the flour and salt into a bowl. Gradually add the eggs, beating until smooth. Add the water, brandy and sesame oil.

Lightly oil a heavy-based pan and place over a high heat until hot. Drop in 3 or 4 tablespoons of batter, spacing them well apart, and cook, as separate small pancakes, until golden and bubbly. Turn and cook the other side of each pancake until golden. Repeat with the remaining batter. Stack the pancakes on a plate between sheets of greaseproof paper and keep warm over a pan of gently simmering water.

Skin and then bone the chicken breasts and slice diagonally into thin slivers. Coat in the cornflour. Heat the oils in a wok or frying pan, add the chicken in 2 or 3 batches and stir-fry for 3 minutes, pushing the chicken slivers to the side of the pan when cooked. Add the garlic, bamboo shoots and plum sauce. Stir gently and heat through until the mixture is bubbling.

Transfer the chicken mixture to a warmed serving dish. Garnish with the spring onion fans and cucumber strips, and serve with the pancakes.

Serves 4

Chicken with Sesame Seeds

For a really authentic flavour, you could use sesame oil for stir-frying the chicken pieces. You can buy it in most good supermarkets. Serve with some plain boiled rice or cooked egg noodles.

375 g (12 oz) boned, skinned chicken breasts
1 egg white
½ teaspoon salt
2 teaspoons cornflour
2 tablespoons white sesame seeds
2 tablespoons oil

1 tablespoon dark soy sauce
1 tablespoon wine vinegar
½ teaspoon chilli bean sauce
½ teaspoon sesame seed oil
1 tablespoon dry sherry
½ teaspoon roasted Szechuan peppercorns
4 spring onions, chopped

Cut the chicken breasts into 7.5 cm (3 inch) long shreds. Combine the egg white, salt and cornflour in a bowl, then toss with the chicken and mix thoroughly. Leave to stand for 15 minutes.

Dry-fry the sesame seeds in a wok until they are golden brown, then remove from the pan and set aside.

Heat the oil in the wok, add the chicken and stir-fry briskly for 1 minute. Remove with a slotted spoon. Add the soy sauce, vinegar, chilli bean sauce, sesame seed oil, sherry and peppercorns to the wok and bring to the boil. Add the chicken and spring onions and stir-fry briskly for 2 minutes. Sprinkle with the sesame seeds and serve immediately.

Serves 4

left: stir-fried chicken breasts
above: chicken with sesame seeds

Rapid-fried Chicken Livers with Mangetout

To offset the richness of this piquant supper dish, serve with plain boiled nutty brown rice and a refreshingly cool cucumber salad or a simple mixed green salad.

1 tablespoon cornflour

8 tablespoons cold chicken stock or water

1 tablespoon tomato purée or ketchup

1 tablespoon dry sherry or sherry vinegar

2 teaspoons Worcestershire sauce

1 teaspoon lemon juice

2 tablespoons groundnut or vegetable oil

250 g (8 oz) mangetout, cut in half crossways if large

1 small onion, finely sliced

250 g (8 oz) frozen chicken livers, defrosted, dried and cut into 2.5 cm (1 inch) thick slices

1 garlic clove, crushed

freshly ground black pepper

sprigs of parsley, to garnish

Blend the cornflour in a jug with 2 tablespoons of the stock or water, then add the remaining stock or water, the tomato purée or ketchup, sherry or vinegar, Worcestershire sauce and the lemon juice. Stir well to combine.

Heat a wok until hot. Add 1 tablespoon of the oil and heat over a moderate heat until hot. Add the mangetout, increase the heat to high and stir-fry for 2 minutes. Remove the mangetout with a slotted spoon and set aside.

Heat the remaining oil in the wok over a moderate heat. Add the onion and stir-fry for 2 minutes. Add the chicken livers and garlic and stir-fry for 2–3 minutes until the chicken livers lose their pink colour. Pour in the cornflour mixture and then bring to the boil over a high heat, stirring constantly until thickened and glossy.

Lower the heat, add plenty of ground black pepper and simmer gently for 5 minutes or until the chicken livers are cooked but still pink in the centre.

Return the mangetout to the wok, increase the heat and toss over a high heat until hot and evenly combined with the livers. Serve at once, garnished with parsley.

Serves 3–4

Chicken with Peppers and Sweetcorn

1 tablespoon oil

3 spring onions, chopped

2 pieces of fresh root ginger, peeled and shredded

500 g (1 lb) boned, skinned chicken breasts, shredded

2 tablespoons light soy sauce

2 tablespoons dry sherry

2 green peppers, cored, deseeded and sliced

425 g (14 oz) can whole baby sweetcorn or kernels, drained

Heat the oil in a wok or frying pan, add the spring onions and ginger and fry for 1 minute. Add the chicken and brown lightly.

Pour in the soy sauce and sherry and cook for a further 1 minute. Stir in the green peppers and sweetcorn and stir-fry for 2 minutes. Pile the mixture onto a warmed serving dish and serve immediately.

Serves 4–6

left: rapid-fried chicken livers with mangetout
below: *chicken with peppers and sweetcorn*

Balinese Roasted and Stir-fried Duck

50 g (2 oz) salted macadamia nuts
2 large garlic cloves, crushed
1 teaspoon ground coriander
½ teaspoon grated fresh root ginger
250 ml (8 fl oz) chicken stock
1 x 2 kg (4 lb) oven-ready duck
250 ml (8 fl oz) boiling water
2 tablespoons oil
2 green chillies, deseeded and finely
  chopped
1 tablespoon lemon juice
salt
To garnish:
sprigs of coriander
chilli powder

Combine the nuts, garlic, coriander, ginger and 25 ml (1 fl oz) of the stock in a food processor or electric blender. Liquidize to a smooth paste, adding a little more stock if the mixture is too dry. Cover and then set aside.

Pierce the duck all over with a fork, then place on a rack in a roasting pan and pour in the boiling water. Cook in a preheated oven, 220°C (425°F), Gas Mark 7, for 45 minutes.

Remove the pan from the oven and pour away the fat and juices. Return the duck to the oven and cook for 45 minutes, or until cooked. Let the duck cool slightly. Remove all the fat, skin and bones and discard. Cut the duck meat into bite-sized pieces.

Heat the oil in a wok or large frying pan over a high heat. Add the nut mixture and stir-fry for 30 seconds. Add the duck and chillies and stir-fry for 1 minute. Blend in the remaining stock, lemon juice and salt. Stir-fry for 5 minutes until the sauce is slightly thickened. Garnish with coriander sprigs and chilli powder and serve immediately.

Serves 4

Quick-fried Ribbons of Duck with Plum and Ginger Sauce

1 tablespoon groundnut or
  vegetable oil
375 g (12 oz) duckling breast fillets,
  skin and fat removed, cut into thin
  strips
250 g (8 oz) red plums, halved,
  stoned and cut into thin strips
4 tablespoons chicken stock or water
1 tablespoon hoisin sauce
2 teaspoons orange juice
2 teaspoons granulated sugar
1 teaspoon soy sauce
½ teaspoon ground ginger
¼ teaspoon Chinese five-spice
  powder
spring onion slices, to garnish

Heat the wok until hot. Add the oil and heat over a moderate heat until hot. Add the duckling, increase the heat to high and stir-fry for 4–5 minutes. Remove the duckling with a slotted spoon and set aside.

Add the plums to the wok with the stock or water, hoisin sauce, orange juice, sugar, soy sauce, ginger and five-spice powder. Stir-fry to mix, then lower the heat and simmer for about 10 minutes or until the plums are soft.

Return the duckling to the wok, increase the heat to high and boil rapidly until the duckling is tender and glazed with the sauce. Serve at once, garnished with spring onion slices.

Serves 2–3

Singaporean Almond Chicken

1 red onion, thinly sliced
1 tablespoon soy sauce
1 tablespoon dry sherry or sherry
  vinegar
1 teaspoon sesame oil
½ teaspoon Chinese five-spice powder
375 g (12 oz) chicken thighs, boned,
  skinned and cut into 1 cm (½ inch)
  pieces
25 g (1 oz) drum dried sliced
  mushrooms
2 teaspoons cornflour
8 tablespoons cold chicken stock or
  water

1 teaspoon tomato purée

125 ml (4 fl oz) vegetable oil for shallow-frying

50 g (2 oz) whole blanched almonds

125 g (4 oz) lean sliced cooked ham, cut into thin strips

250 g (8 oz) can sliced bamboo shoots, drained

Whisk the onion in a bowl with the soy sauce, sherry or vinegar, sesame oil and five-spice powder. Add the pieces of chicken and stir well. Cover and leave to marinate in a cool place for 20–30 minutes, turning the chicken occasionally.

Meanwhile, cook the dried mushrooms in boiling water for about 10 minutes, according to the instructions on the drum. Drain. Blend the cornflour in a jug with 2 tablespoons of the stock or water, then add the remaining stock or water and the tomato purée. Stir well to combine.

Heat the vegetable oil in a wok until hot. Add the almonds and shallow-fry until golden brown. Lift them out with a slotted spoon and then drain on kitchen paper.

Carefully pour all but 1 tablespoon of oil out of the wok. Add the chicken and marinade and

stir-fry over a high heat for 2–3 minutes. Pour in the cornflour mixture and bring to the boil over a high heat, stirring constantly until thickened and glossy. Add the mushrooms with the ham and bamboo shoots. Stir-fry for 1–2 minutes until the chicken is tender and all the ingredients are evenly combined. Serve at once, topped with the fried almonds.

Serves 4

above: quick-fried ribbons of duck with plum and ginger sauce; Singaporean almond chicken

Duck with Almonds

500 g (1 lb) lean duck meat

2 slices fresh root ginger, peeled and
   shredded

1 garlic clove, crushed

3 tablespoons oil

3–4 dried Chinese mushrooms
   (optional)

4 spring onions, sliced

125 g (4 oz) canned bamboo shoots,
   drained and sliced

3 tablespoons soy sauce

2 tablespoons sherry

2 teaspoons cornflour

25 g (1 oz) flaked almonds, toasted

Cut the duck into small chunks and
place in a bowl with the ginger and
garlic. Pour over 1 tablespoon of the
oil and leave to marinate in a cool
place for 30 minutes.

Soak the mushrooms in warm
water for 15 minutes, if using.
Squeeze dry, discard the hard stalks
and then slice the mushroom caps.

Heat the remaining oil in a wok
or deep frying pan, add the spring
onions and stir-fry for 30 seconds.

Add the duck and then cook for 2
minutes. Add the mushrooms,
bamboo shoots, soy sauce and
sherry and cook for 2 minutes.

Blend the cornflour with 1
tablespoon water and stir into the
wok. Cook for 1 minute, stirring,
until thickened. Stir in the toasted
almonds and serve immediately.

Serves 4–6

below: duck with almonds
right: oriental duckling

Oriental Duckling

2 kg (4 lb) oven-ready duckling

5 tablespoons oil

1 large onion, thinly sliced

125 g (4 oz) button mushrooms, thickly sliced

1 garlic clove, crushed

1 small red pepper, cored, deseeded and cut into thin strips

1 small green pepper, cored, deseeded and cut into thin strips

250 g (8 oz) fresh bean sprouts

1 tablespoon soy sauce

1 tablespoon cornflour

2–3 teaspoons dry sherry

300 ml (½ pint) chicken stock

125 g (4 oz) blanched almonds, toasted

salt and pepper

Weigh the duckling and calculate the cooking time at 30 minutes per 500 g (1 lb). Prick the duckling all over with a fork and then place in a roasting tin. Sprinkle with salt and roast in a preheated oven, 190°C (375°F), Gas Mark 5, for the calculated cooking time until golden brown and cooked through. Leave to cool, then strip the flesh and skin from the carcass and cut into thin strips.

Heat 2 tablespoons of the oil in a wok or large frying pan. Add the onion, mushrooms, garlic and peppers and stir-fry for 4 minutes.

Remove from the wok with a slotted spoon, transfer to a plate and keep warm. Heat the remaining oil in the wok, add the duck meat and skin and bean sprouts and stir-fry for 3 minutes. Remove from the wok and keep warm.

Blend the soy sauce with the cornflour and sherry, and stir into the stock. Stir into the wok and bring to the boil, then lower the heat and simmer for 2 minutes. Stir in the almonds and return the cooked ingredients to the wok. Check the seasoning and then heat through for 3 minutes. Serve at once with boiled rice and crisp fried noodles, if liked.

Serves 4

Duck with Orange and Bean Sprouts

pared rind of ½ orange

1 tablespoon cornflour

6 tablespoons water

1 tablespoon dry sherry or sherry
   vinegar

1 tablespoon orange juice

1 tablespoon soy sauce

2 teaspoons hoisin sauce

1 teaspoon soft dark brown sugar

seeds of 6 cardamom pods,
   crushed

2 tablespoons groundnut or
   vegetable oil

1 garlic clove, crushed

2.5 cm (1 inch) piece of fresh root
   ginger, peeled and cut into
   thin strips

375 g (12 oz) duckling breast fillets,
   skin and fat removed, cut into thin
   strips

250 g (8 oz) bean sprouts

segments of 1 orange

Cut the orange rind into matchstick strips, blanch in boiling water for 1 minute, then drain, rinse and pat dry with kitchen paper.

Blend the cornflour in a jug with 2 tablespoons of the water, then add the remaining water, the sherry or vinegar, orange juice, soy and hoisin sauces, sugar and cardamom seeds. Stir well to combine.

Heat a wok until hot. Add the oil and heat over a moderate heat until hot. Add the garlic and ginger and stir-fry for a few seconds. Add the duckling, increase the heat to high and stir-fry for 3–4 minutes. Pour in the cornflour mixture and bring to the boil over a high heat, stirring constantly until thickened and glossy. Stir-fry for 3 more minutes, then add the bean sprouts and orange rind and stir-fry for 1 minute or until the duckling is tender. Add the orange segments and heat through for 30 seconds. Serve at once.

Serves 2–3

below: duck with orange and bean sprouts

Turkey with Piquant Pepper Sauce

This sauce, with its chillies, Szechuan peppercorns and garlic, is not for the faint-hearted! Szechuan peppercorns are available from the spice racks of large supermarkets. They give a tangy, almost citrus, flavour to Chinese food.

1 tablespoon Szechuan peppercorns
3 tablespoons vegetable oil
500 g (1 lb) turkey breast fillets, cut
  into thin strips
3 dried red chillies, finely chopped
3 garlic cloves, crushed
5 cm (2 inch) piece of fresh root
  ginger, peeled and finely chopped
Sauce:
4 teaspoons cornflour
8 tablespoons cold chicken stock or
  water
2 tablespoons white wine vinegar
2 tablespoons soy sauce
1 tablespoon chilli sauce
2 teaspoons soft brown sugar
2 teaspoons tomato purée

Prepare the sauce. Mix the cornflour to a paste with 2 tablespoons of the stock or water, then stir in the remaining stock or water and the rest of the ingredients. Set aside.

Heat a wok until hot. Add the Szechuan peppercorns and then dry-fry over a gentle heat for 1–2 minutes. Remove from the wok and crush in a mortar and pestle.

Heat 2 tablespoons of the oil in the wok over a moderate heat until hot. Add the turkey and Szechuan pepper, increase the heat to high and then stir-fry for 3–4 minutes or until lightly coloured on all sides. Remove the wok from the heat and transfer the turkey to a plate with a slotted spoon. Set aside.

Return the wok to a moderate heat, add the remaining oil and heat until hot. Add the chillies, garlic and ginger and stir-fry for 2–3 minutes or until softened, taking care not to let the ingredients brown.

Stir the sauce to mix, pour into the wok and increase the heat to high. Stir-fry for a few minutes until the sauce is thickened, then return the turkey and its juices to the wok and toss for 1–2 minutes or until all the ingredients are combined and piping hot. Serve at once.

Serves 3–4

Turkey with Coconut, Ginger and Lime

500 g (1 lb) turkey breast fillets, cut
  into thin strips
100 g (3½ oz) creamed coconut,
  roughly chopped
2 tablespoons vegetable oil
juice of ½ lime
freshly ground black pepper
Marinade:
2.5 cm (1 inch) piece of fresh root
  ginger, peeled and crushed
1 garlic clove, crushed
finely grated rind and juice
  of ½ lime
2 tablespoons soy sauce
2 teaspoons light soft brown sugar
To garnish:
lime slices
chopped fresh coriander leaves

Mix all the marinade ingredients together, add the turkey strips and turn to coat. Cover and set aside for at least 20 minutes.

Make the coconut milk. Put the creamed coconut in a measuring jug, pour in boiling water up to the 300 ml (½ pint) mark and stir to dissolve. Set aside.

Heat the oil in a wok until hot. Add the turkey and its marinade and stir-fry for 3–4 minutes or until lightly coloured on all sides.

Add half of the coconut milk and bring to the boil, stirring, then stir-fry for a few minutes. Lift the turkey out of the sauce with a slotted spoon, arrange on a warmed serving platter, cover and keep hot.

Pour the remaining coconut milk into the wok, then add the lime juice. Increase the heat to high and bring to the boil. Stir for a few minutes longer or until the sauce is thickened. Add black pepper to taste, and then pour over the turkey. Garnish with lime slices and coriander leaves and serve at once.

Serves 3–4

Shredded Turkey with Mixed Vegetables

After soaking the dried mushrooms, don't throw the soaking liquid away, but add it to the sauce ingredients for extra flavour.

75 g (3 oz) flaked almonds
4 tablespoons vegetable oil
500 g (1 lb) turkey breast fillets, cut into thin strips
3 medium carrots, diagonally sliced
5–15 g (¼–½ oz) dried shiitake mushrooms, soaked in warm water for 20 minutes, drained and chopped
375 g (12 oz) broccoli florets, trimmed and divided into small sprigs
½ bunch spring onions, diagonally sliced
2 teaspoons sesame oil
freshly ground black pepper
Sauce:
2 teaspoons cornflour
6 tablespoons water
4 tablespoons soy sauce
4 tablespoons rice wine or dry sherry

First prepare the sauce. Mix the cornflour to a thin paste with the water, then stir in the soy sauce and rice wine or sherry. Set aside.

Heat a wok until hot. Add the almonds and dry-fry over a gentle heat until golden brown. Remove and set aside. Add 2 tablespoons of the vegetable oil to the wok and heat over a moderate heat until hot. Add the turkey strips, increase the heat to high and stir-fry for 3–4 minutes or until lightly coloured on all sides. Remove the wok from the heat and tip the turkey and its juices into a bowl. Set aside.

Return the wok to a moderate heat, add the remaining oil and heat until hot. Add the carrots, dried mushrooms and broccoli stalks and stir-fry for 3–4 minutes. Add the broccoli florets and spring onions and then stir-fry for a further 30 seconds.

Stir the sauce to mix, then pour into the wok. Increase the heat to high and stir gently until the sauce thickens, then return the turkey and its juices to the wok and toss for 1–2 minutes or until all the ingredients are combined and piping hot. Add pepper to taste and serve, sprinkled with sesame oil and almonds.

Serves 3–4

Turkey Chow Mein

Chow mein was invented by Chinese immigrants in San Francisco. It is a very good way of using up leftover cooked meat, ham and poultry, especially around Christmastime. The noodles are often deep-fried for chow mein, but this recipe uses boiled noodles, which are a healthier alternative.

250 g (8 oz) packet Chinese rice noodles
2 tablespoons groundnut or vegetable oil
3–4 spring onions, thinly sliced
2.5 cm (1 inch) piece of fresh root ginger, peeled and chopped
1 garlic clove, crushed
250 g (8 oz) skinned and boned cooked turkey, cut into thin strips
200 g (7 oz) Chinese leaves, shredded
200 g (7 oz) bean sprouts
125 g (4 oz) lean sliced cooked ham, cut into thin strips
250 g (8 oz) can sliced bamboo shoots, drained
salt and pepper
Sauce:
2 teaspoons cornflour
8 tablespoons cold chicken stock or water
2 tablespoons soy sauce
2 teaspoons sesame oil

Cook the rice noodles according to packet instructions. Drain the noodles, rinse under cold running water and set aside.

Meanwhile, prepare the sauce. Blend the cornflour in a jug with 2 tablespoons of the stock or water, then add the remaining stock or water, the soy sauce and sesame oil. Stir well to combine.

Heat a wok until hot. Add the oil and heat over a moderate heat until hot. Add the spring onions, ginger and garlic and stir-fry over a gentle heat for 2–3 minutes to blend the flavours without browning the ingredients. Add the turkey, increase the heat to high and stir-fry for 2–3

2–3 minutes. Add the Chinese leaves and bean sprouts and stir-fry for 1–2 minutes until tender-crisp, then add the ham and bamboo shoots and stir-fry to mix.

Pour in the sauce mixture and bring to the boil over a high heat, stirring constantly until thickened and glossy. Fold in the drained noodles, toss over a high heat until hot, then add salt and pepper to taste. Serve at once.

Serves 4

Diced Turkey with Celery

4 Chinese dried mushrooms
375 g (12 oz) boned, skinned turkey
 breast, diced
1 egg white, lightly beaten
1 tablespoon cornflour
4 tablespoons oil
2 garlic cloves, sliced
2 slices fresh root ginger, peeled and
 finely chopped
2 leeks, diagonally sliced
1 small head celery, diagonally sliced
1 red pepper, cored, deseeded and
 sliced
3 tablespoons light soy sauce
2 tablespoons dry sherry
salt
celery leaves, to garnish

Soak the mushrooms in warm water for 15 minutes. Squeeze dry, discard the hard stalks and then slice the mushroom caps.

Season the diced turkey with salt, dip in the egg white and then coat with cornflour. Heat the oil in a wok. Add the turkey and stir-fry for 1 minute until golden brown. Remove with a slotted spoon and then drain on kitchen paper.

Increase the heat, add the garlic, ginger, leeks and celery and stir-fry for 1 minute. Return the turkey to the wok, add the red pepper and stir-fry for 30 seconds. Stir in the soy sauce and sherry and cook for a further 30 seconds. Spoon into a warmed serving dish, garnish with celery leaves and serve immediately.

Serves 4

left: diced turkey with celery

Meat

Ginger Beef with Peppers

Although really lean fillet steak is best for this recipe as it is so tender and cooks very quickly, you could easily substitute sirloin or rump steak instead. Just cut off any fat and then slice or shred really thinly.

500 g (1 lb) lean fillet steak, thinly sliced
2 teaspoons soy sauce
2 tablespoons sesame oil
2.5 cm (1 inch) piece of fresh ginger root, peeled and sliced
2 teaspoons vinegar
1 tablespoon water
1 teaspoon salt
1 teaspoon cornflour
1 garlic clove, crushed
pinch of five-spice powder
1 red pepper, cored, deseeded and cut into chunks
1 green pepper, cored, deseeded and cut into chunks

Put the slices of fillet steak in a bowl and add the soy sauce, 1 teaspoon of the sesame oil, the sliced ginger root, vinegar, water, salt and cornflour. Stir well to mix, until the steak slices are coated thoroughly. Cover the bowl and then leave in the refrigerator to marinate for at least 20 minutes.

Heat the remaining sesame oil in a wok or frying pan and add the garlic and five-spice powder. Stir-fry for 30 seconds and then add the marinated steak slices. Stir-fry quickly for about 2 minutes until the meat is browned on the outside yet still pink and tender on the inside. Remove the steak with a slotted spoon and set aside.

Add the chunks of red and green pepper to the wok or frying pan, and stir-fry briskly for 2–3 minutes, tossing them in the oil. Add the strips of steak and any remaining marinade. Stir-fry for 1 minute until the meat is heated through. Transfer the beef and pepper mixture to a warm serving dish and serve immediately.

Serves 3–4

Stir-fried Beef with Peppers

1 tablespoon olive oil
1 onion, thinly sliced
1 large garlic clove, cut into thin strips
500 g (1 lb) fillet steak, cut into thin strips
1 red pepper, cored, deseeded and cut into matchstick strips
1 green pepper, cored, deseeded and cut into matchstick strips
1 tablespoon soy sauce
2 tablespoons dry sherry
1 tablespoon chopped fresh rosemary
salt and pepper
brown rice, to serve

Heat the olive oil in a wok or a deep frying pan and stir-fry the onion and garlic for 2 minutes. Add the strips of beef and stir-fry briskly for 2–3 minutes until evenly browned on all sides and almost tender. Add the strips of red and green pepper and stir-fry for a further 2 minutes.

Add the soy sauce, sherry, some salt and pepper to taste and the rosemary, and stir-fry for a further 1–2 minutes. Transfer to a warmed serving dish and serve piping hot with plain boiled brown rice.

Serves 6

right: ginger beef with peppers

Peking Beef

375 g (12 oz) rump steak

1 egg white

2 teaspoons cornflour

1 teaspoon mustard powder

½ teaspoon Chinese five-spice powder

2 tablespoons groundnut or
   vegetable oil

6 celery sticks, diagonally sliced

Sauce:

2 teaspoons cornflour

6 tablespoons water

2 tablespoons soy sauce

1 tablespoon red or white wine
   vinegar

1 tablespoon soft dark or light brown
   sugar

1 tablespoon tomato purée

2 teaspoons mustard powder

¼ teaspoon salt

Wrap the rump steak and place in
the freezer for about 1 hour or until
just frozen, and then cut into thin
strips across the grain, discarding
any fat. Lightly beat the egg white
in a shallow dish with the
cornflour, mustard and five-spice
powder. Add the strips of steak and
turn to coat. Set aside.

Prepare the sauce. In a jug, blend
the cornflour with 2 tablespoons of
the water, then add the remaining
water and the remaining sauce
ingredients. Stir well to combine.

Heat a wok until hot. Add 1
tablespoon oil and heat over a
moderate heat until hot. Add the
celery and stir-fry for 2 minutes,
then remove with a slotted spoon
and set aside.

Heat the remaining oil in the
wok. Add about one-quarter of the
meat, increase the heat to high and
stir-fry for 2–3 minutes until
browned on all sides. Remove with
a slotted spoon and set aside on a
plate. Repeat with the remaining
meat, stir-frying it in batches.

Pour the sauce mixture into the
wok and bring to the boil over a
high heat, stirring constantly until
thickened and glossy. Return the
meat and any juices and the celery
to the wok and stir-fry for about 30
seconds or until coated in the sauce.
Serve at once.

Serves 4

above: Peking beef
right: Szechuan shredded beef

Szechuan Shredded Beef

Szechuan dishes come from the western region of China, and are characterized by rich, spicy flavours and the frequent inclusion of chillies. The seeds of the chillies are the hottest part, so include as few, or as many, as you like.

250 g (8 oz) rump or flash-fry steak
1 tablespoon Szechuan peppercorns
2 tablespoons soy sauce
1 tablespoon dry sherry or sherry vinegar
1 tablespoon hoisin sauce
1 tablespoon soft dark brown sugar
½ teaspoon Chinese five-spice powder
2 tablespoons groundnut or vegetable oil
2 green chillies, thinly sliced, seeds discarded if liked
425 g (14 oz) can whole baby sweetcorn, drained, or 250 g (8 oz) fresh whole baby sweetcorn
275 g (9 oz) can bean sprouts, drained, or 175 g (6 oz) fresh bean sprouts
250 g (8 oz) can sliced bamboo shoots, drained

Wrap the steak and place in the freezer for about 1 hour or until just frozen, and then cut into thin strips, across the grain if using rump steak, discarding any fat and sinew.

Crush the Szechuan peppercorns in a pestle and mortar or with the end of a straight wooden rolling pin, then mix in a jug with the remaining ingredients, except the oil, chillies and vegetables.

Heat a wok until hot. Add the oil and heat over a moderate heat until hot. Add the meat, increase the heat to high and stir-fry for 2–3 minutes until browned on all sides. Add the chillies and stir-fry for a few seconds.

If using fresh baby sweetcorn blanch in boiling salted water for 3–4 minutes before using. Add all of the vegetables to the wok, and then the Szechuan pepper mixture. Stir-fry for 2–3 minutes or until the flavours are well blended and the vegetables are hot. Serve at once.

Serves 3–4

Beef in Oyster Sauce

Oyster sauce is used extensively as a flavouring in Chinese cookery. It is made from soy sauce and oysters and has a very characteristic taste and aroma.

250 g (8 oz) sirloin or rump steak
2 tablespoons oyster sauce
1 tablespoon dry sherry
1 tablespoon cornflour
125 g (4 oz) broccoli
125 g (4 oz) bamboo shoots
1 carrot, peeled
125 g (4 oz) button mushrooms or
　3–4 Chinese dried mushrooms
4 tablespoons oil
2 slices of fresh ginger root, peeled
　and chopped
2 spring onions, chopped
1 teaspoon salt
1 teaspoon sugar
2 tablespoons clear beef stock or
　water

Remove any fat or sinew from the rump or sirloin steak and then cut the meat into thickish slices, across the grain. In a bowl, mix together the oyster sauce, sherry and cornflour, and add the steak. Cover and leave in a cool place to marinate in this mixture for about 20 minutes.

Cut the broccoli into small florets. Slice the bamboo shoots and carrot into slices, about the same size as the steak slices. If using Chinese dried mushrooms, soak them in warm water for 20 minutes, squeeze dry, discard the stalks and finely slice the mushrooms.

Heat half of the oil in a wok or a heavy frying pan. Add the steak and then stir-fry over a high heat for 10–15 seconds. Remove with a slotted spoon and set aside.

Heat the remaining oil in the wok and then add the ginger root and spring onions. Stir-fry for 1 minute and then add the rest of the vegetables. Add the salt and sugar and stir-fry for 1½ minutes. Add the steak, stir well and moisten with a little stock or water. Heat through and serve immediately.

Serves 4

Stir-fried Sesame Beef

A mixture of light and dark soy sauces are used in this recipe. Salty soy sauce is made from fermented soya beans, flour and water and is the most commonly used seasoning agent in both Chinese and Japanese cookery.

375 g (12 oz) rump steak
1 tablespoon light soy sauce
1 tablespoon dark soy sauce
1 tablespoon soft light brown sugar
1 teaspoon sesame oil
1 tablespoon dry sherry
2 tablespoons white sesame seeds
2 tablespoons oil
1 garlic clove, thinly sliced
2 celery sticks, diagonally sliced
2 carrots, diagonally sliced
50 g (2 oz) button mushrooms, sliced

Trim any fat and sinew from the steak and then cut into thin slices, across the grain. Combine the soy sauces, sugar, sesame oil and sherry in a bowl. Add the steak slices and toss together. Cover and leave to marinate in the refrigerator or a cool place for 15 minutes.

Dry-fry the sesame seeds in a wok or pan until they are golden brown. Remove from the wok and set aside.

Heat the oil in the wok, add the garlic, celery and carrots and stir-fry briskly for 1 minute. Remove from the wok and reserve.

Increase the heat, add the beef and stir-fry for about 3 minutes until well browned. Return the vegetables to the wok, add the mushrooms and stir-fry briskly for a further 30 seconds.

Spoon the sesame beef mixture into a warmed serving dish, sprinkle with the sesame seeds and serve immediately.

Serves 3–4

right: beef in oyster sauce

Sautéed Calves' Liver with Sherry and Sage

2 tablespoons dry sherry

2 tablespoons Worcestershire sauce

1 teaspoon chopped fresh sage or ½ teaspoon dried sage

2 slices calves' liver, total weight 175–250 g (6–8 oz), cut into thin strips

2 tablespoons olive oil

1 Spanish onion, thinly sliced

2 teaspoons plain flour

75 ml (3 fl oz) dry white wine

salt and pepper

fresh sage leaves, to garnish

Whisk the sherry in a shallow dish with the Worcestershire sauce and sage. Add the strips of calves' liver and turn to coat. Cover and leave to marinate for about 20 minutes, turning the liver occasionally.

Heat a wok until hot. Add the oil and heat over a moderate heat until hot but not smoking. Add the onion slices and then stir-fry for 5 minutes until softened. Remove with a slotted spoon and set aside.

Add the strips of calves' liver and stir-fry over a moderate heat for 1–2 minutes until browned on all sides. Remove the liver with a slotted spoon and set aside.

Sprinkle the flour into the wok and stir-fry until golden brown. Gradually stir in the wine and any marinade from the liver. Bring to the boil over a high heat, stirring constantly, then lower the heat, return the liver to the wok and simmer for a further 2–3 minutes until tender.

Add the onions and salt and pepper to taste, then increase the heat to high and toss to combine. Serve immediately, sprinkled with fresh sage leaves.

Serves 2

Beef Rendang

Blocks of creamed coconut are available in most supermarkets in packets ready for dissolving in boiling water.

2 garlic cloves, chopped
2.5 cm (1 inch) piece of fresh root
   ginger, peeled and chopped
2 dried red chillies
150 g (5 oz) creamed coconut
450 ml (¾ pint) boiling water
1 teaspoon turmeric
½ teaspoon salt
500 g (1 lb) rump steak, trimmed of
   fat and sinew and cut into bite-
   sized chunks
1 bay leaf
To garnish:
desiccated coconut
bay leaves

Pound the garlic and ginger with the chillies in a pestle and mortar or with the end of a straight wooden rolling pin. Dissolve the creamed coconut in the boiling water to make coconut milk, then stir in the turmeric and salt.

Put the steak and the pounded mixture in a wok. Pour in the coconut milk and bring to the boil over a moderate heat, stirring constantly. Lower the heat, add the bay leaf and simmer gently for about 30 minutes or until the sauce is thick, stirring frequently to prevent it sticking to the wok.

Increase the heat to high and stir-fry for at least 10 minutes, until the oil separates out from the coconut sauce. Continue stir-frying until the rendang is quite dry. Discard the bay leaf. Serve hot, sprinkled with desiccated coconut and garnished with bay leaves.

Serves 4

Sizzling Steak with Mango

The contrast between the peppery hotness of the stir-fried beef and the refreshingly cool mango makes this dish tantalising to the taste buds. For a change, melon, papaya or pineapple can be substituted for the mango.

375 g (12 oz) fillet steak
4 black peppercorns
4 tablespoons olive or walnut oil
3 tablespoons dark rum
2 tablespoons lime juice
2 tablespoons chilli sauce
¼ teaspoon ground mixed spice
1 ripe mango
pinch of salt

Wrap the steak and place in the freezer for about 1 hour or until just frozen, and then cut into thin strips across the grain, discarding any fat and sinew. Crush the peppercorns in a pestle and mortar or grind in a pepper mill.

Whisk 2 tablespoons of the oil in a bowl with the rum, lime juice, chilli sauce, crushed peppercorns and mixed spice. Add the slices of steak and stir well to mix. Cover the bowl and leave in a cool place or the refrigerator to marinate for about 4 hours, turning the meat occasionally.

About 15 minutes before cooking, prepare the mango. Peel with a knife, then cut a slice lengthways from each side of the fruit, taking the knife as close to the central stone as possible. Slice these 2 pieces of mango thinly, then cut as much flesh as possible away from the stone and slice this neatly.

Heat a wok or deep frying pan until hot. Add the remaining oil and heat over a moderate heat until hot but not smoking. Add the steak and marinade, increase the heat to high and stir-fry for 2 minutes or until the steak is browned on all sides. Add the mango slices and salt and stir-fry for about 30 seconds or until heated through. Serve at once.

Serves 4

left: sautéed calves' liver with sherry and sage; beef rendang; sizzling steak with mango

Beef with Cashew Nuts

500 g (1 lb) lean fillet steak

2 tablespoons soy sauce

1 tablespoon dry sherry

3 tablespoons sesame oil

3 tablespoons water

2 teaspoons cornflour

1 tablespoon finely chopped peeled
   fresh ginger root

2 garlic cloves, crushed

125 g (4 oz) unsalted roasted
   cashew nuts

3 celery sticks, diagonally sliced

salt and pepper

Cut the fillet steak into thin slices, removing any fat. Place in a bowl and add the soy sauce, dry sherry, 2 teaspoons of the sesame oil, the water, cornflour, seasoning and ginger. Cover and leave in the refrigerator to marinate for at least 20 minutes.

Heat the remaining sesame oil in a deep wok or a heavy frying pan. Remove the strips of steak from the marinade and stir-fry quickly in the hot oil for 2 minutes, until brown and sealed on the outside. Remove and set aside. Reserve the marinade.

Add the garlic, cashew nuts and celery to the wok or frying pan, and then stir-fry quickly over moderate heat for 2–3 minutes, tossing well.

Return the steak to the wok with the reserved marinade and mix well with the cashew nuts and celery. Increase the heat and continue cooking, stirring all the time, until the sauce thickens. Transfer the mixture to a warm serving dish and serve immediately with some boiled rice or noodles.

Serves 3–4

below: beef with cashew nuts
right: beef and mangetout stir-fry

Beef and Mangetout Stir-fry

25 g (1 oz) fresh root ginger, peeled and shredded

1 garlic clove, crushed

4 tablespoons light soy sauce

2 tablespoons dry sherry

1 teaspoon chilli sauce

1 teaspoon clear honey

½ teaspoon Chinese five-spice powder

375 g (12 oz) fillet steak, finely sliced

250 g (8 oz) dried low-fat egg noodles

250 g (8 oz) mangetout, trimmed

salt and pepper

shredded spring onions, to garnish

Combine the ginger, garlic, soy sauce, sherry, chilli sauce, honey and five-spice powder in a non-metallic bowl. Stir well. Add the steak, stir to coat thoroughly, then cover and marinate in a cool place for at least 30 minutes.

Bring a large saucepan of lightly salted water to the boil. Add the noodles, then remove the pan from the heat, cover and leave to stand for 5 minutes.

Meanwhile, heat a wok or frying pan. Add 2 tablespoons of the marinade and the beef and stir-fry for about 3–6 minutes. Add the mangetout and the remaining marinade, with salt and pepper to taste. Stir-fry for 2 minutes.

Drain the noodles and arrange them in warm serving bowls. Spoon the stir-fried beef mixture over the top and then serve garnished with shredded spring onions.

Serves 4

Stir-fried Beef with Celery and Walnuts

Orange julienne looks good as a garnish on this tasty stir-fry. Simply remove the rind from an orange with a vegetable peeler, and then cut into very thin matchstick strips. Blanch the orange rind in boiling water for 1 minute, rinse in cold water and pat dry.

375 g (12 oz) rump or flash-fry steak
1 large orange
2 teaspoons cornflour
4 tablespoons cold beef stock or water
4 tablespoons orange juice
2 teaspoons Worcestershire sauce
2 teaspoons tomato purée
2 tablespoons groundnut or vegetable oil
1 onion, sliced thinly
4 celery sticks, diagonally sliced
50 g (2 oz) walnut pieces
salt and pepper
celery leaves, to garnish

Wrap the steak and place in the freezer for about 1 hour or until just frozen, then cut into thin strips, across the grain if using rump steak, discarding any fat and sinew.

Remove the skin and all the pith from the orange, and then cut between the membranes to divide the orange neatly into segments.

Blend the cornflour in a jug with 1 tablespoon of the stock or water, and then add the remaining stock or water, the orange juice, Worcestershire sauce and tomato purée. Stir well to combine.

Heat a wok until hot. Add the oil and heat over a moderate heat until hot. Add the onion and celery and stir-fry over a gentle heat until slightly softened. Add the meat, increase the heat to high and stir-fry for 3–5 minutes until browned on all sides. Pour in the cornflour

mixture and bring to the boil over a high heat, stirring constantly until thickened and glossy. Remove from the heat and stir in the orange segments, walnuts and salt and pepper to taste. Garnish with celery leaves and serve at once.

Serves 4

Teriyaki Beef Stir-fry

Teriyaki marinade is a bottled Japanese sauce made from naturally brewed soy sauce, wine and spices.

500 g (1 lb) fillet steak
5 cm (2 inch) piece of fresh root ginger, peeled and chopped
3 garlic cloves, chopped
6 black peppercorns
6 tablespoons teriyaki marinade
4 tablespoons sweet sherry
2 tablespoons caster sugar
2 tablespoons groundnut or vegetable oil
1 spring onion, green part only, diagonally sliced, to garnish

Wrap the steak and place in the freezer for about 1 hour or until just frozen, and then cut into thin strips across the grain, discarding any fat.

Crush the ginger and garlic with the peppercorns in a pestle and mortar. Whisk the ginger, garlic and peppercorns in a bowl with the teriyaki marinade, sherry and sugar.

Add the slices of steak and stir well to mix. Cover and leave to marinate in the refrigerator for 24 hours, turning the meat occasionally.

When ready to cook, allow the meat to come to room temperature for about 1 hour. Heat a wok or deep frying pan until hot. Add the oil and heat over a moderate heat until hot. Remove the meat from the marinade with a slotted spoon, add to the wok and increase the heat to high. Stir-fry for 1 minute, then pour over the marinade. Stir-fry for 1 minute until the mixture is hot. Garnish with the spring onion and serve at once.

Serves 4

Stir-fried Beef with Nasturtium Salad

This is a colourful and unusual main course dish, which looks stunning but is not difficult to prepare. Nasturtium flowers are usually available during the summer months. You can buy them in supermarkets or grow them yourself.

2 oranges
500 g (1 lb) lean, prime casserole steak, cut into thin strips
1 teaspoon soy sauce
1 teaspoon medium dry sherry
1 cm (½ inch) piece of fresh root ginger, peeled and grated

½ teaspoon soft brown sugar
1 teaspoon cornflour
1 head chicory, trimmed
8 nasturtium flowers
1 tablespoon sesame oil

Finely grate the rind and squeeze the juice from one orange. Place the beef strips in a bowl and sprinkle over the grated rind and juice. Mix together the soy sauce, sherry, ginger, sugar and cornflour. Pour over the beef, tossing the strips to coat them well. Cover the bowl and chill in the refrigerator for 30 minutes. Drain the beef, reserving the marinade.

Arrange the chicory leaves on 4 serving plates. Peel the remaining orange, removing all the white pith. Carefully remove the orange segments from the membrane. Arrange the orange over the chicory leaves and top with 2 nasturtium flowers on each plate.

Heat the oil in a wok or a large frying pan and then stir-fry the beef strips over a high heat for 2 minutes. Pour over the marinade and cook for a further 1 minute. Spoon the beef on to the serving plates and serve immediately.

Serves 4

left: stir-fried beef with celery and walnuts; teriyaki beef stir-fry

Steak in Oyster Sauce

This is a classic Cantonese dish. Bottled oyster sauce is rich, dark in colour and highly concentrated in flavour. It is made from oysters, soy sauce and brine.

500 g (1 lb) rump or flash-fry
   steak
2 garlic cloves, crushed
3 tablespoons soy sauce
2 tablespoons dry sherry or sherry
   vinegar
2 teaspoons cornflour
1 teaspoon caster sugar
2 tablespoons groundnut or
   vegetable oil
300 g (10 oz) Chinese leaves,
   finely shredded
5 spring onions, diagonally sliced
2.5 cm (1 inch) piece of fresh root
   ginger, peeled and cut into
   matchsticks
½ teaspoon salt
2 tablespoons oyster sauce
freshly ground black pepper

Wrap the steak and place in the freezer for about 1 hour or until just frozen, and then cut into thin slices, across the grain if using rump steak, discarding any fat and sinew.

Whisk the garlic in a bowl with the soy sauce, sherry or vinegar, cornflour, sugar and plenty of pepper. Add the slices of steak and stir well to mix. Cover and leave to marinate in the refrigerator or a cool place for 20–30 minutes,

turning the steak over occasionally in the marinade.

Heat a wok until hot. Add 1 tablespoon oil and heat over a moderate heat until hot. Add the Chinese leaves, spring onions, ginger and salt and stir-fry for 1½ minutes or until the Chinese leaves are just beginning to wilt. Remove the Chinese leaf mixture with a slotted spoon and keep warm.

Heat the remaining oil in a wok. Remove about one-quarter of the steak from the marinade with a slotted spoon and add to the wok. Increase the heat to high and stir-fry for 2–3 minutes until the meat is browned on all sides. Remove with

a slotted spoon and set aside on a plate. Repeat with the remaining steak, stir-frying it in batches.

Add the oyster sauce and the marinade to the wok and bring to the boil over a high heat, stirring until thickened and glossy. Return the steak and the Chinese leaf mixture to the wok and stir-fry for 30 seconds or until evenly combined and coated in the sauce. Serve at once.

Serves 4

below: steak in oyster sauce
right: pineapple beef

Return all the steak and juices to the wok, pour in the cornflour mixture and bring to the boil over a high heat, stirring constantly until thickened and glossy. Add the pineapple and spring onions and stir-fry for about 30 seconds or until heated through. Garnish with parsley sprigs and serve at once.

Serves 4

Pineapple Beef

When fresh pineapple is not in season, you can use canned sliced pineapple in natural juice instead.

500 g (1 lb) rump steak
2.5 cm (1 inch) piece of fresh root
   ginger, peeled and chopped
3 tablespoons oil
2 tablespoons soy sauce
2 teaspoons soft dark brown sugar
¼ teaspoon Chinese five-spice powder
2 teaspoons cornflour
4 tablespoons cold beef stock or
   water
2 tablespoons dry sherry or sherry
   vinegar
4 slices fresh pineapple, cut into thin
   chunks
½ bunch spring onions, diagonally
   sliced into 1 cm (½ inch) lengths
parsley sprigs, to garnish

Wrap the steak and place in the freezer for about 1 hour or until just frozen, and then cut into 5 cm (2 inch) long slices across the grain, discarding any fat and sinew.

Whisk the ginger in a bowl with 1 tablespoon oil, 1 tablespoon soy sauce, the sugar and five-spice powder. Add the steak and stir well. Cover and leave to marinate for 20–30 minutes, stirring occasionally.

Blend the cornflour in a jug with 1 tablespoon of the stock or water, then add the remaining stock or water, the sherry or vinegar and the remaining soy sauce. Stir well.

Heat a wok until hot. Add the remaining oil and heat over a moderate heat until hot. Add about one-quarter of the steak and then increase the heat to high. Stir-fry for 2–3 minutes until the steak is browned on all sides. Remove with a slotted spoon and set aside on a plate. Repeat with the remaining steak, stir-frying it in batches.

Sizzling Beef

2 tablespoons vegetable oil
6 spring onions, diagonally sliced
4 celery sticks, diagonally sliced
500 g (1 lb) rump or fillet steak, cut
   into thin strips
4 tablespoons beef stock or water
2 tablespoons sherry vinegar
2 tablespoons Worcestershire sauce
2 teaspoons tomato purée
salt and pepper

Heat a wok until hot. Add the oil and heat over a moderate heat until hot. Add the spring onions and celery and stir-fry for 2–3 minutes or until slightly softened. Add the steak strips, increase the heat to high and stir-fry for 3–4 minutes until browned on all sides.

Add the stock or water, sherry vinegar, Worcestershire sauce, tomato purée and salt and pepper to taste. Stir-fry over a high heat until sizzling. Serve at once.

Serves 3–4

and drain on absorbent kitchen paper.

Heat the remaining oil in the wok. Add the vegetables, increase the heat to high and stir-fry for 2 minutes. Add the steak mixture and remaining teriyaki marinade, then stir-fry for 30 seconds. Throw in the cashews and stir-fry for a further 30 seconds or until all the ingredients are heated through and evenly mixed. Season to taste and serve at once.

Serves 4

Beef Chow Mein

250 g (8 oz) vermicelli
1 tablespoon vegetable oil
25 g (1 oz) butter
2 tablespoons sunflower oil or sesame
seed oil
375 g (12 oz) frying steak, cut into
thin strips
8 spring onions, sliced
1 garlic clove, crushed
1 red pepper, cored, deseeded and
thinly sliced
1 green pepper, cored, deseeded and
thinly sliced
125 g (4 oz) button mushrooms,
sliced
1 tablespoon cornflour
2 tablespoons light soy sauce
2 tablespoons sherry
150 ml (¼ pint) vegetable or beef stock
1 tablespoon sesame seeds
salt
spring onion tassels, to garnish

Stir-fried Beef with Cashews and Mangetout

375 g (12 oz) flash-fry steak
4 tablespoons walnut oil
1 garlic clove, crushed
5 tablespoons teriyaki marinade
100 g (3½ oz) packet unsalted
cashew nuts
125 g (4 oz) mangetout
1 large green or red pepper, cored,
deseeded and cut lengthways into
thin strips
4 spring onions, diagonally sliced into
4 cm (1½ inch) lengths
salt and pepper

Wrap the steak and place in the freezer for about 1 hour or until just frozen, and then cut into thin slices. Heat a wok or frying pan until hot. Add 2 tablespoons oil and heat over a moderate heat until hot but not smoking. Add the steak, increase the heat to high and stir-fry for 2–3 minutes until the steak is browned on all sides.

Transfer the steak to a bowl with a slotted spoon. Add the garlic and 3 tablespoons teriyaki marinade to the steak and stir well to mix. Leave to cool.

Add 1 tablespoon oil to the wok and heat as before. Add the cashews and stir-fry for 1–2 minutes until golden brown, then remove from the oil with a slotted spoon

Cook the vermicelli in plenty of boiling salted water, to which the vegetable oil has been added, until just tender. Drain the vermicelli, rinse with hot water and drain well. Melt the butter in the saucepan and toss the vermicelli to coat evenly.

Heat the sunflower or sesame seed oil in a wok or large frying pan, add the steak and stir-fry quickly for 2 minutes. Remove the steak from the wok, using a slotted spoon, and place on a plate. Add the spring onions, garlic, red and green peppers and mushrooms to the wok and stir-fry quickly for 1–2 minutes.

Blend together the cornflour, soy sauce and sherry and add to the wok with the stock. Bring to the boil, stirring, and then cook for 1 minute. Add the vermicelli and combine well with the stir-fried steak and vegetables.

Arrange the beef chow mein in a warmed serving dish, sprinkle with sesame seeds and garnish with spring onion tassels. Serve with stir-fried vegetables.

Serves 4

Note: To make spring onion tassels, cut the green ends off spring onions and slit the remainder in a cross down to the bulb. Place in a bowl of iced water until the leaves unfurl and form tassels.

far left: stir-fried beef with cashews and mangetout
right: stir-fried chilli beef

Stir-fried Chilli Beef

500 g (1 lb) rump steak, cut across the grain into thin slices
2 tablespoons oil
2 dried red chillies
2 garlic cloves, thinly sliced
1 cm (½ inch) piece of fresh root ginger, peeled and shredded
4 spring onions, shredded
2 tablespoons dark soy sauce
2 tablespoons light soy sauce
2 tablespoons dry sherry
2 green chillies, deseeded and chopped
salt

Season the steak slices well with salt. Heat the oil in a wok or a deep frying pan, add the dried red chillies and stir-fry for 1 minute. Remove from the wok.

Increase the heat, add the steak to the wok and stir-fry for 1 minute until browned. Add the garlic, ginger and spring onions and cook for 30 seconds. Pour over the soy sauces and sherry, add the green chillies and cook for a further minute. Transfer the stir-fried mixture to a warmed serving dish and serve immediately.

Serves 4

Beef with Pak Choi in Oyster Sauce

A classic dish from the Cantonese region of China. Pak choi, sometimes also called Chinese cabbage, is excellent in stir-fries. It has a crisp texture, is juicy when bitten into and has a mild mustard flavour. Take care not to overcook it or you will lose its best qualities. If you are unable to obtain it, Swiss chard can be substituted.

500 g (1 lb) rump or fillet steak, cut
   into thin strips
3 tablespoons vegetable oil
300 g (10 oz) pak choi, shredded
5 spring onions, diagonally sliced
2.5 cm (1 inch) piece fresh root
   ginger, peeled and chopped
½ teaspoon salt
2 tablespoons oyster sauce
pepper
Marinade:
2 garlic cloves, crushed
3 tablespoons soy sauce
2 tablespoons rice wine or dry sherry
1 teaspoon caster sugar

Make the marinade. Put the garlic in a shallow dish with the soy sauce, rice wine or sherry and sugar. Add the beef strips and turn to coat. Cover and leave to marinate for about 30 minutes, turning the meat occasionally.

Heat a wok until hot. Add 2 tablespoons of the oil and heat over a moderate heat until hot. Add the beef and its marinade, increase the heat to high and stir-fry for 3–4 minutes or until browned on all sides. Remove the wok from the heat and tip the beef and its juices into a bowl. Set aside.

Return the wok to a moderate heat. Add the remaining oil and heat until hot. Add the pak choi, spring onions, ginger and salt and stir-fry for 1–2 minutes or until the pak choi is just starting to wilt.

Return the beef and its juices to the wok, add the oyster sauce and increase the heat to high. Toss until all the ingredients are evenly combined. Add pepper to taste and serve at once.

Serves 3–4

Stir-fried Orange Beef

375 g (12 oz) rump steak
2 teaspoons sesame oil
2 tablespoons dark soy sauce
1 tablespoon dry sherry
1 cm (½ inch) piece fresh root ginger,
   peeled and finely chopped
2 teaspoons cornflour
4 tablespoons oil
2 dried red chillies, crumbled
shredded rind of 1 orange
pinch of salt
½ teaspoon roasted Szechuan
   peppercorns, finely ground
1 teaspoon light soft brown sugar
orange slices and parsley sprigs, to
   garnish

Cut the beef into thin slices 5 cm (2 inches) long, cutting against the grain. Combine half of the sesame oil, half of the soy sauce, the sherry, ginger and cornflour. Add the steak and toss until well coated. Cover and leave in a cool place to marinate for 15 minutes and then drain well.

Heat the oil in a wok and quickly brown the steak on all sides for 2 minutes, then drain on kitchen paper. Pour off all but 1 tablespoon oil from the wok.

Heat the wok, add the chillies and stir-fry for 30 seconds. Return the steak to the wok, add the orange rind, salt, pepper, sugar and remaining soy sauce. Stir-fry for 4 minutes, sprinkle with the remaining sesame oil and serve immediately, garnished with the orange slices and parsley sprigs.

Serves 4

Hot and Sour Pork

Protein-packed tofu makes a little meat go a long way in this colourful dish. Vegetables are included too, so the only accompaniment needed is boiled rice.

375 g (12 oz) pork fillet (tenderloin)
3 tablespoons soy sauce

2 tablespoons cider vinegar

2 teaspoons cornflour

2.5 cm (1 inch) piece of fresh root ginger, peeled

1 large garlic clove

2 dried red chillies, roughly chopped

300 g (10 oz) packet tofu, drained and dried

4 tablespoons oil

1 large red pepper, cored, deseeded and cut lengthways into strips

250 g (8 oz) mangetout

125 ml (4 fl oz) chicken stock

1–2 tablespoons chilli sauce

salt and pepper

coriander sprigs, to garnish

Wrap the pork and place in the freezer for about 1 hour or until just frozen, then cut on the diagonal into 5 mm (¼ inch) thick slices. Place the slices in a bowl, add the soy sauce, vinegar and cornflour and stir well to mix. Set aside.

Pound the ginger and garlic using a pestle and mortar or process in a food processor or blender with the chillies. Cut the tofu into slices roughly the same size as the pork.

Heat a wok or frying pan until hot. Add 1 tablespoon oil and heat over a moderate heat until hot. Add the red pepper and mangetout, season with salt and pepper and stir-fry for 3 minutes. Remove with a slotted spoon and set aside.

Heat 2 tablespoons oil in the wok, add the tofu and stir-fry carefully over a moderate heat for 1–2 minutes until lightly coloured on both sides. Remove with a slotted spoon, then drain on kitchen paper and keep hot.

Heat the remaining oil in the wok, add the pounded mixture and stir-fry over a gentle heat for 2–3 minutes to blend the flavours without browning the ingredients. Add about half of the pork, increase the heat to high and stir-fry for 2–3 minutes. Remove and set aside while you cook the remaining meat.

Pour the stock into the wok and bring to the boil over a high heat, stirring constantly, and then stir in the chilli sauce. Return the pork to the wok with the red pepper and mangetout. Stir-fry for 1–2 minutes until all the ingredients are hot and evenly combined. Gently fold in the tofu, garnish with coriander and serve at once.

Serves 4

below: hot and sour pork

Stir-fried Pork with Cucumber

In this unusual recipe, the pork is stir-fried with pieces of cucumber and flavoured with aromatic root ginger.

375 g (12 oz) pork fillet (tenderloin)
1 cucumber
1 tablespoon cornflour
150 ml (¼ pint) chicken stock
   or water
2 tablespoons soy sauce
2 tablespoons dry sherry or sherry
   vinegar
1 tablespoon vegetable oil
1 onion, thinly sliced
2.5 cm (1 inch) piece of fresh root
   ginger, peeled and cut into
   matchsticks
salt and pepper

Wrap the pork and place in the freezer for about 1 hour or until just frozen. Trim away any fat and then cut the meat on the diagonal into 5 mm (¼ inch) thick slices, and then cut the slices into thin strips.

Trim off the ends of the cucumber and cut it into 6 equal pieces. Cut each of these pieces into quarters lengthways and then scoop out and discard the seeds.

Blend the cornflour in a jug with 2 tablespoons of the stock or water, then add the remaining stock or water, the soy sauce and sherry or vinegar. Stir well to combine.

Heat a wok or deep frying pan until hot. Add the oil and heat over a moderate heat until hot. Add the onion and ginger and stir-fry for a few seconds, then add the pork, increase the heat to high and stir-fry for 2–3 minutes.

Pour in the cornflour mixture and bring to the boil over a high heat, stirring constantly until the sauce has thickened and is glossy.

Add the cucumber and stir-fry for 1–2 minutes or until the meat is tender and the cucumber is hot. Add salt and pepper to taste and serve at once.

Serves 4

Pork with Peas

This recipe is more French than oriental in flavour, but the pork and vegetables are stir-fried in a wok or a deep, heavy frying pan in the usual way.

375 g (12 oz) pork fillet (tenderloin)
1 tablespoon olive oil or
   vegetable oil
1 Spanish onion, quartered and thinly
   sliced
1 tablespoon tomato purée
2 teaspoons paprika, plus extra,
   to garnish
½ teaspoon chilli powder
¼ teaspoon caster sugar
125 ml (4 fl oz) dry white wine
250 g (8 oz) frozen petits pois
2 garlic cloves, crushed
2 tablespoons chopped coriander or
   parsley
salt and pepper

Wrap the pork and place in the freezer for about 1 hour or until it is just frozen. Trim away and discard any fat and then cut the meat on the diagonal into 5 mm (¼ inch) thick slices.

Heat a wok or a deep frying pan until hot. Add the oil and heat over a moderate heat until hot. Add the pork and onion slices, increase the heat to high and stir-fry for 2–3 minutes. Remove with a slotted spoon and set aside on a plate.

Remove the wok from the heat and add the tomato purée, paprika, chilli powder and sugar. Stir well to combine and then gradually stir in the wine. Return the wok to the heat, bring to the boil, stirring, then add the frozen peas, garlic and salt and pepper to taste. Lower the heat and simmer for 5 minutes or until the peas are cooked and the sauce has reduced, stirring frequently.

Return the pork and onion mixture to the wok, together with any juices, and increase the heat to high. Stir-fry for 1–2 minutes until the meat is tender and coated in the sauce mixture. Remove from the heat, stir in the coriander or parsley and serve at once, sprinkled with paprika.

Serves 4

right: pork with peas; stir-fried pork with cucumber

Ants Climbing Trees

This dish gets its name from the minced pork (ants) clinging to the noodles (trees). Transparent cellophane noodles are the traditional noodles used, but we have substituted ordinary egg noodles which are just as good.

250 g (8 oz) minced pork
200 g (7 oz) packet fine egg noodles
2 tablespoons groundnut oil or vegetable oil
4 spring onions, trimmed and chopped
250 ml (8 fl oz) hot chicken stock
2 spring onions, finely chopped, to garnish

Marinade:
2 tablespoons soy sauce
1 tablespoon dry sherry or sherry vinegar
1 tablespoon groundnut oil or vegetable oil
1 teaspoon sesame oil
1 teaspoon chilli sauce
½ teaspoon sugar
pinch of salt

Whisk the marinade ingredients together in a bowl. Add the minced pork and stir well to mix. Cover and leave to marinate for about 30 minutes. Meanwhile, cook the noodles, according to the packet instructions, and drain thoroughly.

Heat a wok or a deep frying pan until hot. Add the oil and heat over a moderate heat until hot. Add the pork and spring onions and stir-fry for about 5 minutes or until the meat loses its pink colour. Pour in the stock and bring to the boil, stirring constantly, then add the drained noodles.

Stir-fry for 1 minute or until all of the liquid is absorbed and the noodles are hot. Sprinkle with the spring onions and serve at once.

Serves 3–4

Paper-thin Lamb with Garlic and Spring Onions

500 g (1 lb) lamb neck fillet
2 tablespoons groundnut oil or vegetable oil
3 large garlic cloves, thinly sliced
½ teaspoon chilli powder, or to taste
½ teaspoon soft dark brown sugar
pinch of salt
1 large bunch spring onions, cut into 7 cm (3 inch) lengths, then shredded lengthways
2 tablespoons soy sauce
2 tablespoons dry sherry or sherry vinegar
2 teaspoons sesame oil

Wrap the lamb and place in the freezer for about 1 hour or until just

frozen, then cut into thin strips across the grain, discarding any fat.

Heat a wok or a deep frying pan until hot. Add the oil and heat over a moderate heat until hot. Add the garlic and stir-fry over a gentle heat for a few seconds to flavour the oil, then add the lamb and sprinkle over the chilli powder, sugar and salt. Increase the heat to high and stir-fry for 3–4 minutes until the lamb is browned on all sides.

Add the spring onions, the soy sauce and sherry or vinegar, then stir-fry for 1–2 minutes or until the lamb is tender and all the ingredients are quite dry. Serve at once, sprinkled with the sesame oil.

Serves 4

Pork Chow Mein

500 g (1 lb) egg noodles
300 g (10 oz) pork fillet, cut into
    matchstick strips
3 teaspoons cornflour
2 tablespoons soy sauce
1 tablespoon dry sherry
1 teaspoon salt
1 teaspoon sugar
5 tablespoons groundnut oil
125 g (4 oz) bamboo shoots, cut into
    matchstick strips
½ cucumber, cut into matchstick strips
125 g (4 oz) spinach, shredded
1 teaspoon dark sesame oil

Bring a saucepan of water to the boil, add the noodles and simmer for 5 minutes until soft but not sticky. Drain thoroughly and rinse with cold water.

Mix the pork with 2 teaspoons of the cornflour. Mix together the soy sauce, sherry, salt, sugar and the remaining cornflour.

Heat half of the groundnut oil in a wok. Place the noodles in a large bowl, separating them with a fork. Pour over the hot oil, stirring to coat. Return the noodles to the wok, stir-fry for 2–3 minutes, and then place on a serving dish.

Heat the remaining groundnut oil and stir-fry the bamboo shoots, cucumber, spinach and pork for 3 minutes. Add the soy sauce mixture and stir until thickened. Pour the mixture over the noodles, sprinkle with the sesame oil and then serve immediately.

Serves 4

far left: ants climbing trees
above: pork chow mein

Oriental Pork with Tofu

Take care when stir-frying tofu (bean curd) as it has a tendency to break up, especially around the edges.

250 g (8 oz) pork fillet (tenderloin)
2 tablespoons groundnut or
   vegetable oil
2 garlic cloves, crushed
300 g (10 oz) packet tofu, drained,
   dried and cut into cubes
250 g (8 oz) mooli, peeled and cut
   into matchsticks
125 g (4 oz) mangetout
250 g (8 oz) Chinese leaves, shredded
1 teaspoon sesame oil
Sauce:
2 teaspoons cornflour
6 tablespoons cold chicken stock or
   water
2 tablespoons soy sauce
2 tablespoons dry sherry or sherry
   vinegar
2 teaspoons lemon juice
½ teaspoon Chinese five-spice powder
½ teaspoon chilli power, or to taste
pinch of salt

Wrap the pork and place in the freezer for about 1 hour, or until just frozen. Cut on the diagonal into 5 mm (¼ inch) thick slices, and then cut the slices into thin strips.

Prepare the sauce. In a jug, blend the cornflour with 2 tablespoons of the stock or water, then add the remaining stock or water and the remaining ingredients. Stir well.

Heat a wok or deep frying pan until hot. Add the oil and heat over a moderate heat until hot. Add the pork and garlic, increase the heat to high and stir-fry for 2–3 minutes. Remove and set aside on a plate.

Add the tofu to the wok and stir-fry carefully over a moderate heat for about 1–2 minutes until lightly coloured on all sides. Remove with a slotted spoon, drain on kitchen paper and keep hot.

Add the mooli and mangetout to the wok and stir-fry for 2 minutes, then add the Chinese leaves and stir-fry for 1 minute longer. Pour in the sauce mixture and bring to the boil over a high heat, stirring constantly until thickened and glossy. Return the pork and any juices to the wok and stir-fry for 1–2 minutes until the pork is tender and evenly combined with the vegetables. Gently fold in the tofu and serve at once, sprinkled with the sesame oil.

Serves 4

Lamb with Walnuts and Yellow Bean Sauce

500 g (1 lb) lamb neck fillet
2 tablespoons groundnut or
   vegetable oil
1 large Spanish onion, quartered and
   thinly sliced
2 large garlic cloves, crushed
4 tablespoons yellow bean sauce
50 g (2 oz) walnut pieces
salt and pepper

Wrap the lamb and then place in the freezer for about 1 hour, or until just frozen. Remove from the freezer and cut into thin strips across the grain, discarding any fat.

Heat a wok until hot. Add the oil and heat over a moderate heat until hot. Add the onion and stir-fry for 2–3 minutes until softened. Add the lamb and garlic, increase the heat to high and stir-fry for 3–4 minutes until the lamb is well browned.

Add the yellow bean sauce and salt and pepper to taste, then toss the lamb for 1–2 minutes until tender and coated in the sauce. Stir in the walnuts, stir-fry for 30 seconds and then serve hot.

Serves 4

Szechuan Pork

Szechuan dishes are hot and spicy, so include as many of the fresh chilli seeds in this dish as you dare!

500 g (l lb) pork fillet (tenderloin)
3 tablespoons groundnut or
    vegetable oil
1 green pepper, cored, deseeded and
    cut lengthways into strips
2.5 cm (1 inch) piece of fresh root
    ginger, peeled and chopped
2 garlic cloves, finely chopped
2 fresh green chillies, deseeded and
    chopped
250 g (8 oz) can sliced bamboo
    shoots, drained
Sauce:
2 teaspoons cornflour
6 tablespoons cold chicken stock or
    water
2 tablespoons chilli sauce
2 tablespoons dry sherry or sherry
    vinegar
1 tablespoon soy sauce
2 teaspoons soft dark brown
    sugar
pinch of salt

Wrap the pork and place in the freezer for about 1 hour or until just frozen. Trim off and discard any fat and cut the meat on the diagonal into 5 mm (¼ inch) thick slices, then cut the slices into thin strips.

Prepare the sauce. In a jug, blend the cornflour with 2 tablespoons of the stock or water, then add the remaining stock or water and the rest of the sauce ingredients. Stir well to combine.

Heat a wok or a deep frying pan until hot. Add the oil and heat over a moderate heat until hot. Add the pork, increase the heat to high and then stir-fry briskly for 2–3 minutes. Remove the pork with a slotted spoon and set aside on a plate.

Add the green pepper, ginger, garlic and chillies and stir-fry for 1 minute, then pour in the sauce mixture and bring to the boil over a high heat, stirring constantly until thickened and glossy.

Return the pork and any juices to the wok with the bamboo shoots and stir-fry over a high heat for 1–2 minutes until the pork is tender and the bamboo shoots are hot. Transfer to a serving dish and serve at once.

Serves 4

far left: lamb with walnuts and yellow bean sauce
below: *oriental pork with tofu*

Lamb's Liver with Leeks and Spring Onions

1 teaspoon cornflour

1 tablespoon soy sauce

½ teaspoon Chinese five-spice powder

¼–½ teaspoon chilli powder, according to taste

250 g (8 oz) lamb's liver, cut into 4 cm x 5 mm (1½ x ¼ inch) strips

2 tablespoons groundnut oil or vegetable oil

1 garlic clove, crushed

2 leeks, shredded

4 spring onions, shredded

salt and pepper

Sauce:

2 teaspoons cornflour

2 tablespoons water

2 tablespoons dry sherry or sherry vinegar

2 teaspoons soy sauce

1 teaspoon caster sugar

1 teaspoon sesame oil

Whisk the cornflour in a bowl with the soy sauce, five-spice powder and chilli powder. Add the strips of liver and turn to coat. Cover and leave to marinate for 30 minutes.

Prepare the sauce. Blend the cornflour in a jug with the water, then add the sherry or vinegar, soy sauce, sugar and sesame oil. Stir well to combine.

Heat a wok until hot. Add half the oil and heat over a moderate heat until hot. Add the liver and garlic and stir-fry for 2–3 minutes until the liver is browned on all sides. Remove and set aside.

Heat the remaining oil in the wok. Add the leeks and spring onions and stir-fry for 1 minute. Pour in the sauce mixture and bring to the boil over a high heat, stirring until thickened and glossy. Return the liver to the wok and add salt and pepper to taste. Stir-fry for 30 seconds or until the liver is evenly coated in the sauce. Serve at once.

Serves 2

Yellow Flower Lamb

375 g (12 oz) lamb neck fillet

2 eggs

4 spring onions, finely chopped

2½ tablespoons groundnut oil or vegetable oil

15 g (½ oz) dried sliced mushrooms

2.5 cm (1 inch) piece of fresh root ginger, peeled and finely chopped

½ x 175 g (6 oz) can sliced bamboo shoots, drained

2 tablespoons soy sauce

2 tablespoons dry sherry or sherry vinegar

1 teaspoon soft dark brown sugar

½ teaspoon Chinese five-spice powder

1 tablespoon sesame oil

salt and pepper

Wrap the lamb and place in the freezer for about 1 hour or until just frozen. Cut on the diagonal into thin strips, discarding any fat.

Beat the eggs in a bowl with half of the spring onions and salt and pepper to taste. Heat 1½ teaspoons of the oil in a pan and make a flat omelette with the egg mixture. Slide the omelette out of the pan on to a plate and roll up tightly. Set aside.

Soak the dried mushrooms in boiling water for 10 minutes and then drain.

Heat the remaining oil in a wok or a deep frying pan until hot. Add the remaining spring onions and the ginger and stir-fry over a gentle heat for a few seconds to flavour the oil. Add the lamb, increase the heat to high and stir-fry for 2–3 minutes until browned on all sides. Add the mushrooms, bamboo shoots, soy sauce, sherry or vinegar, sugar and five-spice powder. Stir-fry for 1–2 minutes or until the lamb is tender and all the ingredients are hot and evenly combined.

Transfer the stir-fried lamb mixture to a warmed serving dish. Slice the rolled omelette into thin rings, and then arrange on top of the lamb to resemble flower petals. Sprinkle over the sesame oil and serve at once.

Serves 4

left: yellow flower lamb; Szechuan pork (see page 65); lamb's liver with leeks and spring onions

Fish and Shellfish

Squid and Green Peppers

If you don't want to clean and prepare the squid yourself, you can ask the fishmonger to do it for you, or even buy it cut into rings and tentacles, either fresh or frozen. If frozen, thaw the squid thoroughly before stir-frying it.

250 g (8 oz) squid
1 green pepper, cored and deseeded
2 slices fresh ginger root, peeled
oil, for deep-frying
1 teaspoon salt
1 tablespoon soy sauce
1 teaspoon vinegar
1 teaspoon sesame oil
pepper

Clean the squid, discarding the head and the transparent back bone as well as the ink bag. Wash well under running cold water and then pat dry with some kitchen paper. Peel off the thin skin of the squid and cut the flesh into small pieces. Slice the green pepper and thinly shred the fresh ginger root.

Heat the oil in a wok or a deep frying pan until it is fairly hot. Deep fry the prepared squid for about 30 seconds and then remove from the wok with a slotted spoon. Carefully pour off the excess oil, leaving about 1 tablespoon of oil in the wok. Add the ginger and green pepper and then return the squid to the wok.

Stir-fry for a few seconds and then stir in the salt, soy sauce, vinegar and pepper. Cook for about 1 minute, and then add the sesame oil and serve.

Serves 2–4

Prawn Noodles with Sesame Sauce

Dried egg noodles are quick and easy to cook and are excellent for bulking out a wide range of stir-fried dishes. Here they are mixed with prawns in a sesame sauce. For a superior flavour, you could use raw king prawns which will be more tender and succulent.

375 g (12 oz) egg noodles
1 teaspoon cornflour
1 egg white
175 g (6 oz) peeled, cooked prawns
3 tablespoons vegetable oil
6 spring onions, cut into strips
2 tablespoons soy sauce
2 tablespoons dry sherry
Sauce:
3 tablespoons sesame paste
6 tablespoons water
2 tablespoons soy sauce
2 tablespoons red wine vinegar
1 teaspoon chilli sauce
1 tablespoon sesame oil
1 garlic clove, crushed
4 spring onions, finely chopped

Cook the egg noodles in plenty of boiling salted water for about 5–6 minutes until just tender. Drain and rinse them with hot water, then drain thoroughly in a sieve.

Beat together the cornflour and egg white to obtain a white froth. Mix in the prawns.

To make the sauce, put the sesame paste into a bowl and gradually mix in the water. Stir in the remaining ingredients.

Heat the oil in a wok or a large frying pan over a high heat. Add the prawns and spring onions, and stir-fry for 1 minute. Stir in the cooked egg noodles, soy sauce and sherry and mix well. Cook, stirring, for a further 2 minutes.

Divide the noodles between 4 warmed serving plates or bowls. Spoon the sesame sauce over the top and serve immediately.

Serves 4

right: squid and green peppers

Soft Noodles with Crab Meat Sauce

150 g (5 oz) egg noodles
2 tablespoons oil
1 small can crab meat, about
 125 g (4 oz) drained weight
125 g (4 oz) spinach or cabbage,
 cut into rough pieces
1 teaspoon soy sauce
250 ml (8 fl oz) vegetable stock
1 spring onion, finely
 chopped

Cook the egg noodles in plenty of boiling salted water for about 5–6 minutes. Drain through a sieve and keep warm in a serving dish.

Heat the oil in a wok or a frying pan and stir-fry the crab meat and spinach or cabbage. Add the soy sauce and stock. Cook for 2–3 minutes, pour the mixture over the noodles, then sprinkle over the spring onion. Serve at once.

Serves 2–3

Quick-fried Squid with Crab and Tomato Sauce

500 g (1 lb) cleaned squid, fresh or
 frozen and thawed
1 tablespoon oil
2 pieces of fresh root ginger, peeled
 and finely chopped
3 spring onions, finely chopped
175 g (6 oz) can crab meat
65 g (2½ oz) can tomato purée
1 teaspoon sugar
1 tablespoon light soy sauce
4 tablespoons chicken stock
1 tablespoon dry sherry
2 teaspoons cornflour
chopped spring onion, to garnish

Cut the squid into 2.5 cm (1 inch) pieces. Heat the oil in a wok or deep frying pan, then add the ginger and spring onions and stir-fry for 1 minute. Add the squid and cook for 2 minutes. Add the remaining ingredients, except the cornflour, and mix well. Stir-fry briskly for 2 more minutes.

Blend the cornflour to a smooth paste with 1 tablespoon water. Stir into the wok or pan and then cook, stirring, until the sauce thickens. Spoon the squid and crab mixture into a warmed serving dish, garnish with spring onion and then serve immediately.

Serves 4–6

Quick-fried Crab in Aromatic Oil

You can buy a cooked crab from the fresh fish counter of most supermarkets. If you don't like the idea of preparing the crab yourself, you may be able to get a dressed crab instead. Canned or frozen crab meat can be substituted in this classic Chinese dish but will not give the same results.

1 large freshly cooked crab
2 tablespoons oil
1 garlic clove, crushed
2 pieces of fresh root ginger, peeled and finely chopped
4 spring onions, chopped
1 leek, thinly sliced
1 egg, beaten
150 ml (¼ pint) fish or chicken stock

2 tablespoons dry sherry
2 teaspoons cornflour, blended with 1 tablespoon water
2 teaspoons sesame seed oil
salt
lemon wedges, to garnish

Break off the legs and crack the claws of the crab. Using a chopper or cleaver, crack the shell into 4 or 5 pieces. Remove all the meat and cut into pieces, discarding the black sac, grey gills and intestinal thread.

Heat the oil in a wok or a deep frying pan, add the garlic, ginger and spring onions and stir-fry for 1 minute. Add the crab and stir-fry for 5 minutes over a high heat. Add the leek and salt to taste.

Lower the heat and pour in the egg in a thin stream. Add the stock and sherry and cook for 1 minute. Add the cornflour and sesame oil. Cook, stirring, until thickened. Turn onto a warmed serving dish and serve immediately, garnished with lemon wedges.

Serves 4–6

Note: Two 175 g (6 oz) cans crab meat may be used in place of fresh crab.

far left: soft noodles with crab meat sauce
above left: quick-fried squid with crab and tomato sauce
above: quick-fried crab in aromatic oil

Crab in Black Bean Sauce

2 tablespoons oil

2 tablespoons salted black beans, coarsely chopped

2 garlic cloves, crushed

2 tablespoons finely chopped fresh root ginger

4 spring onions, chopped

250 g (8 oz) lean finely minced pork

1 large cooked crab, cut into pieces (black sac, gills and intestinal thread discarded)

2 tablespoons dry sherry

300 ml (½ pint) chicken stock, preferably homemade

2 eggs, beaten

1–2 teaspoons sesame oil

spring onion flowers, to garnish (see right)

Heat the oil in a wok, add the black beans, garlic, ginger and spring onions and stir-fry briskly for 30 seconds. Add the pork and brown quickly for 1 minute. Add the crab, sherry and stock and boil rapidly for 8–10 minutes.

Combine the eggs and sesame oil and stir into the wok. Stir for 30 seconds until the egg has cooked into strands. Transfer the crab and pork mixture to a warmed serving dish, garnish with spring onion flowers and serve immediately.

Serves 4

To make spring onion flowers: Trim the green top and remove the white part. Shred the top, leaving 2.5 cm (1 inch) attached at the base. Immerse in iced water until the spring onion opens out and curls.

below: crab in black bean sauce
right: prawns in chilli sauce

Spiced Prawns in Coconut

4 tablespoons oil
1 large onion, sliced
4 garlic cloves, thinly sliced
2 teaspoons ground coriander
1 teaspoon turmeric
1 teaspoon chilli powder
½ teaspoon ground ginger
½ teaspoon salt
2 tablespoons vinegar
200 ml (7 fl oz) coconut milk
2 tablespoons tomato purée
500 g (1 lb) peeled cooked prawns
pepper
To Garnish:
whole cooked prawns in shells
lemon slices

Heat the oil in a wok or a deep frying pan, add the onion and garlic and stir-fry gently until soft and golden brown.

Mix the spices together in a bowl, add the salt and pepper to taste, stir in the vinegar and mix to a paste. Add the spice paste to the wok and stir-fry for 3 minutes, stirring constantly.

Stir in the coconut milk and tomato purée and simmer for 5 minutes. Add the prawns and stir-fry for 2–3 minutes until heated thoroughly and coated in the sauce. Spoon into a warmed serving dish and garnish with whole prawns and lemon slices.

Serves 4

Prawns in Chilli Sauce

1 tablespoon oil
3 spring onions, chopped
2 teaspoons finely chopped fresh root
  ginger
250 g (8 oz) peeled cooked prawns
125 g (4 oz) mangetout
½ teaspoon chilli powder
1 teaspoon tomato purée
¼ teaspoon salt
½ teaspoon sugar
1 tablespoon dry sherry
½ teaspoon sesame oil
whole cooked prawns in shells, to
  garnish

Heat the oil in a wok or a deep frying pan, then add the spring onions and ginger and stir-fry for about 30 seconds. Add the prawns, mangetout, chilli powder, tomato purée, salt, sugar and sherry and stir-fry briskly for 5 minutes.

Sprinkle over the sesame oil and arrange the prawn and vegetable mixture on a warmed serving dish. Serve immediately, garnished with whole prawns.

Serves 3–4

Stir-fried Crab with Pork and Noodles

6 tablespoons sunflower oil

2 eggs

2 fresh red chillies, finely chopped

375 g (12 oz) crab meat

150 g (5 oz) medium or thread egg noodles

1 bunch of spring onions, white and green parts separated and chopped

2.5 cm (1 inch) piece fresh root ginger, peeled and crushed

2 garlic cloves, crushed

3 tablespoons yellow bean sauce

375 g (12 oz) pork fillet, cut diagonally into 3.5 x 1 cm (1½ x ½ inch) strips

200 g (7 oz) mangetout, topped and tailed

150 g (5 oz) fresh bean sprouts

1 red pepper, halved lengthways, cored, deseeded and then cut into thin strips

150 ml (¼ pint) boiling stock, e.g. fish, vegetable or chicken, or water

4 tablespoons soy sauce

salt

Make the omelette to use as a garnish. Heat about 2 teaspoons of the oil in an omelette pan or small, heavy-based frying pan. Beat 1 egg in a bowl with half of the chopped chillies, about 2 tablespoons of the crab meat and a pinch of salt. When the oil is very hot, pour in the egg mixture and let it run to the sides of the pan, drawing the set mixture into the centre with a palette knife. Cook for a few minutes until the omelette is set, then slide it out on to a plate. Make another omelette in the same way, and leave them both to cool.

Bring a large saucepan of water to the boil. Add the noodles, cover the pan, then immediately remove it from the heat. Leave it to stand for 6 minutes, then drain well.

Heat 3 tablespoons of the oil in a wok or a deep, heavy frying pan. Add the chopped white parts of the spring onions, the ginger, garlic and yellow bean sauce. Stir-fry over a gentle heat for 2–3 minutes.

Increase the heat to moderate, add the pork strips and stir-fry for 5 minutes until tender. Remove the spring onion mixture and pork with a slotted spoon and set aside.

Heat the remaining oil in the wok. Add the mangetout, bean sprouts and red pepper and stir-fry over a high heat for 2–3 minutes until they are tender but still crisp.

Return the pork and spring onion mixture to the wok and add the noodles. Pour in the stock or water and the soy sauce and stir-fry until the ingredients are evenly mixed and heated through. Taste the mixture and add salt, if necessary. Transfer to a warm serving platter.

Roll up each omelette into a cigar shape, and cut into thin strips. Sprinkle over the dish together with the reserved green parts of the spring onions. Serve at once.

Serves 4

left: stir-fried crab with pork and noodles
far right: prawns with broccoli

Prawns with Broccoli

250 g (8 oz) cooked king prawns in
their shells

1 slice of fresh ginger root, peeled
and finely chopped

1 tablespoon medium or dry sherry

1 egg white

1 teaspoon cornflour

3 tablespoons vegetable oil

2 spring onions, finely chopped

250 g (8 oz) broccoli, cut into pieces

1 teaspoon salt

1 teaspoon sugar

Wash the king prawns and then dry
thoroughly on kitchen paper. Shell
the prawns and remove the black
intestinal vein. Split each prawn in
half lengthways and then cut into
small pieces.

Put the prawn pieces in a small
bowl with the ginger, sherry, egg
white and cornflour. Stir and leave
in a cool place or the refrigerator to
marinate for about 20 minutes.

Heat 1 tablespoon of the oil in a
wok or a frying pan and add the
prawns. Stir-fry over moderate heat
for about 30 seconds. Remove with
a slotted spoon.

Heat the remaining oil in the
wok or pan. Add the spring onions
and broccoli and stir well. Add the
salt and sugar and stir-fry until the
broccoli is just tender. Mix in the
prawns and serve hot.

Serves 2–3

Stir-fried Prawns with Water Chestnuts and Mangetout

The crisp, nutty texture of the water chestnuts contrasts well with the softness of prawns and the colour combination of all the different ingredients makes this a pretty dish for a dinner party.

2 tablespoons sesame seeds
1 tablespoon groundnut or
   vegetable oil

1 tablespoon sesame oil
1 bunch spring onions, sliced
   diagonally into 2.5 cm (1 inch)
   lengths
5 cm (2 inch) piece of fresh root
   ginger, peeled and chopped
250 g (8 oz) mangetout
½ teaspoon salt
375 g (12 oz) peeled cooked prawns,
   thawed and dried thoroughly if
   frozen
250 g (8 oz) can water chestnuts,
   drained and thinly sliced
3 tablespoons soy sauce
mint sprigs, to garnish

Put the sesame seeds in a wok and dry-fry over a moderate heat for 1–2 minutes until toasted. Remove from the wok and set aside.

Add the groundnut or vegetable oil and the sesame oil to the hot wok. Heat over a moderate heat until hot but not smoking. Add the spring onions, ginger, mangetout and salt and stir-fry for 2 minutes.

Add the prawns, water chestnuts and soy sauce. Increase the heat to high and stir-fry for a further 2 minutes. Garnish with mint sprigs and then serve at once, sprinkled with the toasted sesame seeds.

Serves 4

Scallops in Ginger Cream

1 large pinch of saffron threads
2 tablespoons boiling water
8 shelled scallops, thawed and dried
    thoroughly if frozen
2 tablespoons butter
1 tablespoon groundnut or
    vegetable oil
1 small onion, finely chopped
6 tablespoons dry white wine or dry
    vermouth or sherry
1 piece preserved stem ginger, with
    syrup, finely chopped
150 ml (¼ pint) double cream
salt and pepper
dill or chervil sprigs, to garnish

Put the saffron threads in a small
heatproof bowl. Pour over the
boiling water, stir and leave to soak.
Meanwhile, cut the scallops in half
horizontally, then detach and
reserve the corals.

Heat a wok until hot. Add the
butter and oil and heat gently until
foaming. Add the onion and stir-fry
for 2 minutes or until softened.
Strain in the saffron liquid. Pour in
the wine, vermouth or sherry and
bring to the boil over a high heat,
then stir in the stem ginger.

Add the scallops and stir-fry over
a moderate heat for 3 minutes. Add
the corals, cream and season to
taste. Stir-fry for 1 minute. Serve
hot, sprinkled with dill or chervil.

Serves 4

Squid with Herbs

This is a healthy Mediterranean way of
stir-frying baby squid with aromatic
garlic and herbs. Dishes such as this can
be found in restaurants and bars along
the shores of Spain, Italy and Greece.
Now try making it yourself at home.

1 kg (2 lb) prepared baby squid
4 tablespoons olive oil
3–4 garlic cloves, thickly sliced
2 tablespoons chopped thyme
1 tablespoon chopped parsley
juice of ½ lemon
salt and pepper
lemon slices and tiny bunches of
    thyme, to garnish

Cut the squid into slices and cut the
tentacles in half if they are large.
Heat the oil in a wok, add the garlic
and then cook gently until
browned, then discard. Season the
squid with salt and pepper.

Increase the heat, add the squid
to the wok and cook briskly for just
under 1 minute. Sprinkle with the
herbs and lemon juice. Serve
immediately, garnished with lemon
slices and thyme, and accompanied
by crusty bread.

Serves 4

far left: stir-fried prawns with water
chestnuts and mangetout; scallops in
ginger cream
below: squid with herbs

Noodles with Shrimp Sauce

500 g (1 lb) egg noodles
75 g (3 oz) Chinese mushrooms
2 tablespoons vegetable oil
175 g (6 oz) boned, skinned
   chicken, diced
1 garlic clove, crushed

2 slices of fresh root ginger, peeled
   and chopped
4 spring onions, cut diagonally into
   1 cm (½ inch) pieces
175 g (6 oz) shelled cooked prawns
2 tablespoons soy sauce
2 tablespoons dry sherry
900 ml (1½ pints) fish stock
2 tablespoons cornflour
50 g (2 oz) cooked lean ham, shredded
salt

Bring a large saucepan of salted water to the boil and add the egg noodles. Boil rapidly, according to the package instructions, until they are just tender. Drain and divide the noodles between 6 serving dishes. Keep warm.

While the noodles are cooking, place the dried Chinese mushrooms in a bowl, cover with warm water and leave to soak for 20 minutes.

Drain, reserving the soaking liquid. Discard the stalks and then slice the caps thinly.

Heat the oil in a deep wok or a large saucepan. Add the chicken, garlic and ginger and stir-fry for 2–3 minutes. Add the spring onions and Chinese mushrooms and then stir-fry for 2 minutes.

Add the prawns, soy sauce, sherry, ½ teaspoon salt and the stock. Bring to the boil and then simmer over a gentle heat for 5 minutes. Mix the cornflour with a little water and stir into the liquid in the wok. Keep stirring over a low heat until the mixture thickens slightly. Pour over the noodles, sprinkle with the shredded ham and serve immediately.

Serves 6

Catalan Noodles with Seafood

4 garlic cloves, chopped
1½ tablespoons chopped
  parsley
4 tablespoons olive oil
2 onions, chopped
3 tomatoes, skinned, deseeded and
  chopped
1½ teaspoons paprika
375 g (12 oz) scorpion fish, monkfish
  or halibut, cut into pieces
250 g (8 oz) raw king prawns in their
  shells
1.2 litres (2 pints) rich fish stock

275 g (9 oz) dried vermicelli or
  spaghettini, broken into short
  lengths
large pinch of saffron threads,
  crushed
chopped parsley, to garnish
  (optional)
To serve:
aïoli (garlic mayonnaise)
lemon wedges

Pound the garlic cloves and parsley together. Heat 2 tablespoons of the oil in a deep wok or large frying pan. Add the onions and tomatoes, and cook gently, until softened. Add the garlic and parsley mixture and the paprika. Stir-fry for 2–3 minutes. Stir in all the seafood and coat. Add the stock, bring just to the boil, then simmer gently for 5 minutes.

Meanwhile, heat the remaining oil in a large wok or paella pan, add the pasta and stir over a moderate heat until light golden brown – do not allow to scorch.

Remove the seafood from the wok and keep warm. Pour the contents of the wok on to the pasta, add the saffron and bring to the boil. Boil for 5 minutes or until most of the liquid has been absorbed and the pasta is cooked and tender.

Arrange the seafood on top, then remove from the heat and leave covered by a thick cloth for a couple of minutes before sprinkling with a little parsley, if liked, and serving from the wok or paella pan with aïoli and lemon wedges.

Serves 4

Prawn Chilli Fry

This is a useful standby recipe when you need to rustle up a meal from the freezer in a hurry. However, instead of using frozen prawns you could add some raw shelled king prawns.

3 tablespoons oil
3 onions, sliced
2 green chillies, deseeded and
  chopped
2.5 cm (1 inch) piece of fresh root
  ginger, peeled and chopped
½ teaspoon chilli powder
½ teaspoon turmeric
250 g (8 oz) packet frozen prawns,
  defrosted and dried thoroughly
salt
chopped coriander leaves, to garnish

Heat the oil in a wok or a deep frying pan, add the onions and stir-fry until soft and golden. Add the chillies, ginger, chilli powder, turmeric and some salt to taste, then stir-fry for 2 minutes.

Add the prawns and stir-fry, uncovered, for about 3 minutes or until all the moisture has evaporated. Serve at once, garnished with coriander leaves.

Serves 4

far left: noodles with shrimp sauce

Prawns in Coconut Milk

Coconut 'milk' can be made in many different ways, with fresh coconut, blocks or cans of creamed coconut or with desiccated coconut. This recipe uses desiccated coconut and boiling water, an inexpensive method but deliciously creamy nonetheless.

25 g (1 oz) desiccated coconut
150 ml (¼ pint) boiling water
2 tablespoons groundnut or
    vegetable oil
2 celery sticks, diagonally sliced
4 spring onions, diagonally sliced
1 garlic clove, crushed
1 teaspoon ground coriander
1 teaspoon ground cumin
½ teaspoon ground ginger
½ teaspoon turmeric
½–1 teaspoon chilli powder, according
    to taste
1 tablespoon tomato purée
500 g (1 lb) cooked peeled prawns,
    thawed and dried thoroughly if
    frozen
2 tablespoons chopped fresh mint
½ teaspoon salt or to taste
mint sprigs, to garnish

Put the coconut in a bowl, pour in the boiling water and then stir well to mix. Set aside for 30 minutes.

Heat a wok or a deep frying pan until hot. Add the oil and heat over a moderate heat until hot. Add the celery, spring onions and garlic and stir-fry for 30 seconds. Add the

Honeyed Prawns

1 fresh red chilli

1 fresh green chilli

1 tablespoon groundnut or
   vegetable oil

2.5 cm (1 inch) piece of fresh root
   ginger, peeled and chopped

250 g (8 oz) peeled cooked prawns,
   thawed and dried thoroughly if
   frozen

salt and pepper

Sauce:

2 teaspoons cornflour

4 tablespoons cold fish stock or water

2 tablespoons clear honey

1 tablespoon soy sauce

Slice the chillies crossways into thin rings, and then rinse under cold running water to remove the seeds. Pat dry with kitchen paper.

Prepare the sauce. Blend the cornflour in a jug with 1 tablespoon of the stock or water, then add the remaining stock or water and the rest of the ingredients. Stir well.

Heat a wok until hot. Add the oil and heat over a moderate heat until hot. Add the ginger, chillies and prawns and stir-fry for 30 seconds. Pour in the sauce mixture and bring to the boil over a high heat, stirring constantly until thickened and glossy. Add salt and pepper to taste and serve at once.

Serves 2

---

spices and stir-fry for a further 30 seconds, then remove the wok from the heat.

Pour the coconut mixture into the wok through a fine sieve and press with the back of a metal spoon to extract as much milk as possible. Stir in the tomato purée, return the wok to a high heat and bring to the boil, stirring. Simmer for 5–10 minutes until thickened, stirring frequently.

Add the prawns to the coconut mixture and stir-fry for 1–2 minutes until heated through. Stir in the chopped mint and salt, then taste and add more chilli powder if liked. Serve immediately, garnished with mint sprigs.

Serves 4

far left: prawns in coconut milk
above: honeyed prawns

heated through. Add the reserved corals and then stir-fry for a further minute. Season with salt and pepper to taste and serve at once, garnished with lemon slices or segments.

Serves 2

Haddock in Chilli Sauce

4 tablespoons oil

2 large onions, sliced

3 garlic cloves, crushed

750 g (1½ lb) haddock fillets, skinned, boned and cut into chunks

2 tablespoons plain flour

1 teaspoon turmeric

4 green chillies (deseeded if liked), thinly sliced

2 tablespoons lemon juice

175 ml (6 fl oz) thick coconut milk

salt

chilli flowers, to garnish (optional, see right)

Heat the oil in a wok or a deep frying pan, add the onions and fry until soft and golden. Add the garlic and cook for 30 seconds. Remove from the pan with a slotted spoon and set aside.

Toss the haddock in the flour, add to the wok and brown quickly on all sides. Remove with a slotted spoon and drain on kitchen paper.

Return the onions and garlic to the wok, stir in the turmeric and

Scallops with Lemon and Ginger

8 shelled scallops with corals, thawed and dried thoroughly if frozen

15 g (½ oz) butter

2 tablespoons vegetable oil

½ bunch spring onions, diagonally sliced

½ teaspoon turmeric

3 tablespoons lemon juice

2 tablespoons rice wine or dry sherry

2 pieces stem ginger, with syrup, chopped

salt and pepper

lemon slices or segments, to garnish

Slice the scallops thickly, detaching the corals and keeping them whole. Set the corals aside.

Heat a wok or deep frying pan until hot. Add the butter and 1 tablespoon of the oil and heat over a gentle heat until foaming. Add the sliced scallops and stir-fry for 3 minutes. Remove the wok from the heat and transfer the scallops to a plate with a slotted spoon. Set aside.

Return the wok to a moderate heat, add the remaining oil and heat until hot. Add the spring onions and turmeric and then stir-fry for a few seconds. Add the lemon juice and rice wine or sherry and bring to the boil, then stir in the stem ginger.

Return the scallops and their juices to the wok and toss until chillies and cook for 1 minute. Stir in the lemon juice, coconut milk and salt, and simmer, uncovered, for 10 minutes, stirring until the sauce has thickened. Return the fish to the wok and heat for 2–3 minutes. Spoon into a serving dish and garnish with chilli flowers, if using.

Serves 4

To make chilli flowers: Shred the chilli lengthways, leaving 1 cm (½ inch) attached at the stem end. Place in iced water for about 1 hour to open.

Prawns with Asparagus

175 g (6 oz) fresh asparagus, cut into
   2.5 cm (1 inch) pieces
4 tablespoons dry sherry
1 teaspoon light soy sauce
500 g (1 lb) peeled cooked prawns
2 tablespoons oil
2 garlic cloves, thinly sliced
2 teaspoons finely chopped fresh root
   ginger
4 spring onions, chopped
salt

Blanch the asparagus in a pan of boiling salted water for 2 minutes, then drain well and set aside.

Mix the sherry and soy sauce together in a large bowl. Stir in the prawns and leave to stand in a cool place for 15 minutes.

Heat the oil in a wok and quickly stir-fry the garlic, ginger and half of the spring onions. Add the prawns and marinade and the asparagus and then stir-fry for 1–2 minutes. Transfer to a warmed serving dish and sprinkle with the remaining spring onions. Serve immediately.

Serves 4

Coconut Fish

2 tablespoons oil
4 green chillies, deseeded and
   chopped
2 garlic cloves, finely chopped
2.5 cm (1 inch) piece of fresh root
   ginger, peeled and finely chopped
125 g (4 oz) creamed coconut
1 kg (2 lb) thick haddock fillets,
   skinned and cubed
juice of 2 lemons
salt

Heat the oil in a wok or large frying pan, add the chillies, garlic and ginger and stir-fry gently for 3 minutes. Add the creamed coconut and, when bubbling, stir in the haddock and salt to taste. Stir well.

Cook for 3–4 minutes, stirring and breaking up the haddock as it cooks. As soon as all the fish is cooked through, pour in the lemon juice, stir well and serve.

Serves 4

far left: haddock in chilli sauce
below: prawns with asparagus

Noodles and Rice

Egg-fried Noodles with Vegetable Tofu

vegetable oil, for deep-frying

250 g (8 oz) plain tofu, cubed

75 g (3 oz) dried thread egg noodles

125 g (4 oz) broccoli florets

125 g (4 oz) whole baby sweetcorn, halved

3 tablespoons light soy sauce

1 tablespoon lemon juice

1 teaspoon sugar

1 teaspoon chilli sauce

3 tablespoons sunflower oil

1 garlic clove, chopped

1 red chilli, deseeded and sliced

2 eggs, lightly beaten

125 g (4 oz) drained water chestnuts, sliced

Heat about 5 cm (2 inches) of the vegetable oil in a heavy-bottomed saucepan until a cube of bread browns in 30 seconds. Add the tofu and fry for 3–4 minutes until crisp and lightly golden. Remove and drain the tofu on kitchen paper.

Cook the noodles in a large pan of boiling water, according to the packet instructions, drain, refresh under cold water and dry well on kitchen paper.

Blanch the broccoli florets and sweetcorn in a pan of boiling water for 1 minute. Drain, refresh under cold water and pat dry with kitchen paper. Mix together the soy sauce, lemon juice, sugar and chilli sauce.

Heat the sunflower oil in a wok or large frying pan and stir-fry the garlic and chilli for 3 minutes. Add the noodles and stir-fry for 5 minutes until golden and crisp.

Stir in the eggs and stir-fry for 1 minute, then stir in the sauce, tofu, vegetables and water chestnuts and stir-fry for a further 2–3 minutes until heated through. Serve at once.

Serves 4

Chinese-style Vermicelli

250 g (8 oz) dried vermicelli

4 carrots, cut into fine julienne

4 courgettes, cut into fine julienne

125 g (4 oz) mangetout, trimmed

2 tablespoons groundnut or corn oil

4 spring onions, diagonally sliced

2.5 cm (1 inch) piece of fresh root ginger, peeled and thinly sliced

1–2 garlic cloves, crushed

4 tablespoons soy sauce

1 tablespoon clear honey

1 tablespoon wine vinegar

1 teaspoon coriander seeds, crushed

salt and pepper

parsley leaves, to garnish

Bring a large pan of salted water to the boil. Add the vermicelli, stir and bring back to the boil. Boil for 8–10 minutes, or according to the packet instructions, stirring occasionally.

Meanwhile, put the carrots, courgettes and mangetout in a colander or sieve and sprinkle with salt to taste. Place the colander over the pan of boiling vermicelli. Cover and steam until the vegetables are tender but still crunchy – less than 5 minutes. Remove the colander and set aside. Drain the vermicelli and cut into shorter lengths.

Heat the oil in a wok or a deep frying pan. Add the spring onions and ginger and cook gently, stirring, until the ingredients give off a spicy aroma. Add the garlic, soy sauce, honey, wine vinegar and coriander seeds, stirring well.

Add the lengths of vermicelli and the vegetables. Increase the heat and toss the ingredients in the wok vigorously until they are evenly combined and very hot. Season with pepper to taste. Turn into a warm serving bowl and garnish with parsley leaves. Serve at once.

Serves 4

right: egg-fried noodles with vegetable tofu

Egg Noodles in Yellow Bean and Chilli Sauce

Egg noodles are mainly used in northern China. They are just like pasta, which makes a good substitute. Marco Polo is reputed to have brought the recipe for making them home to Italy after his travels in China.

375 g (12 oz) egg noodles or
   spahgettini
3 tablespoons yellow bean paste
2 teaspoons chilli sauce
1 garlic clove, crushed
3 tablespoons oil
2 green peppers, cored, deseeded
   and sliced
1 onion, thinly sliced
150 g (5 oz) bean sprouts
salt

Cook the noodles or spaghettini in plenty of boiling, salted water until they are tender but just firm to the bite. Drain well. Mix together the yellow bean paste, chilli sauce and garlic.

Heat the oil in a wok or a large frying pan over a high heat. Add the green peppers, onion and bean sprouts and stir-fry for 2 minutes. Add the cooked noodles and stir in the yellow bean and chilli sauce mixture. Heat through and transfer to a warmed serving dish.

Serves 4

Thai Fried Noodles

1 kg (2 lb) boned, skinned chicken
   breasts, cut into 5 mm (¼ inch)
   slices
4 tablespoons dry sherry
6 dried Chinese mushrooms
375 g (12 oz) rice stick noodles
6 tablespoons oil
25 g (1 oz) fresh basil
8 garlic cloves, thinly sliced
6 small onions, thinly sliced
4 red chillies, deseeded and finely
   chopped
1 teaspoon shrimp paste

175 g (6 oz) peeled prawns
3 tablespoons tomato purée
2 tablespoons sugar
1 tablespoon fish sauce (nam pla)
25 g (1 oz) bean sprouts
salt
To garnish:
2 tablespoons roasted peanuts,
   coarsely chopped
½ teaspoon dried red pepper flakes

Toss the chicken with the sherry in a bowl. Cover and then marinate in a cool place for 30 minutes.

Soak the mushrooms in a bowl of warm water for 15 minutes, and the noodles in hot water for 15 minutes. Squeeze the mushrooms, dry them and discard the hard stalks. Thinly slice the mushroom caps. Drain the noodles.

Heat 2 tablespoons of the oil in a wok or frying pan, add half of the basil and stir-fry briefly until crisp. Drain on kitchen paper, and then set aside for the garnish.

Heat 3 tablespoons of the oil in the wok over a moderate heat. Add the garlic and onions, then stir-fry until crisp. Remove from the oil and set aside for a garnish. Pour the oil into a large heatproof bowl, add the drained noodles and toss gently to coat. Set aside.

Combine the chillies, shrimp paste and salt to taste in a mortar and pound until smooth. Heat the remaining oil in a wok or large frying pan over a high heat. Add the chilli mixture and stir-fry for 1 minute. Add the chicken mixture and mushrooms. Stir-fry for 3 minutes. Add the prawns and cook until just heated through. Blend in the tomato purée, sugar and fish sauce. Add the bean sprouts and the remaining basil, then stir-fry briskly for 2 minutes.

Add the noodles in 3 batches, tossing gently after each addition, until thoroughly coated and heated through. Transfer the mixture to a heated serving platter. Sprinkle with the fried basil, garlic and onions, peanuts and pepper flakes. Serve immediately.

Serves 4

Fresh Noodles with Sesame Paste Sauce

Fresh noodles are available at Chinese food stores and they are particularly delicious. Here they are flavoured with an aromatic sesame sauce in hot stock.

500 g (1 lb) fresh noodles
900 ml (1½ pints) chicken stock
Sauce:
2 tablespoons sesame seed paste
4 tablespoons water
4 tablespoons spring onions, chopped
1 teaspoon soy sauce
2 teaspoons red wine vinegar
2 teaspoons chilli oil
1 teaspoon salt

Cook the fresh noodles in plenty of boiling, salted water until they are just tender. Meanwhile, bring the stock to the boil in another pan. When the noodles are cooked, drain well. Divide the boiling stock between 4 individual soup bowls.

Make the sauce. Mix the sesame seed paste and water, and add the remaining ingredients. Add the noodles and top with the sauce.

Serves 4–6

far left: egg noodles in yellow bean and chilli sauce
left: fresh noodles with sesame paste sauce

Chap-chee

375 g (12 oz) fillet or rump steak, trimmed of fat and cut into thin strips

125 g (4 oz) thread egg noodles

3 tablespoons groundnut or corn oil

1 small onion, thinly sliced

2 carrots, cut into fine strips

125 g (4 oz) button mushrooms, sliced

125 g (4 oz) Chinese leaves, shredded

125 g (4 oz) spinach leaves, torn into pieces

salt and pepper

chopped spring onion tops, to garnish

Marinade:

2 tablespoons soy sauce

1 tablespoon groundnut oil

1 tablespoon sesame seeds

1 teaspoon soft brown sugar

1 spring onion, chopped

1 cm (½ inch) piece of fresh root ginger, peeled and crushed

1–2 garlic cloves, crushed

First make the marinade. Mix all the ingredients together in a bowl. Add the steak strips and turn them over to coat them thoroughly. Cover and leave to marinate in a cool place for about 30 minutes.

Bring a large saucepan of water to the boil. Add the egg noodles, cover the pan and immediately remove from the heat. Leave to stand for 6 minutes. Drain the noodles and cut them into 5–7 cm (2–3 inch) lengths with kitchen scissors.

Heat the oil in a wok or a deep, heavy frying pan. Add the steak and marinade and stir-fry over a brisk heat for about 5 minutes until the steak is tender but still pink in the centre. Remove from the wok with a slotted spoon and set aside.

Reduce the heat, add the onion and stir-fry until it has softened and is light golden. Add the carrots and then stir-fry for 3–4 minutes. Add the mushrooms, Chinese leaves and spinach and stir-fry for 1–2 minutes.

Finally return the steak to the wok and add the noodles. Increase the heat to maximum and toss the ingredients together to heat them through. Season with salt and pepper to taste.

Turn into a warm serving bowl, sprinkle over the chopped spring onion tops and serve at once.

Serves 4

Mee Goreng

This quickly prepared Singaporean dish contains tofu (bean curd) which is an excellent source of low-fat protein.

250 g (8 oz) thread egg noodles
4 tablespoons groundnut or corn oil
250 g (8 oz) firm tofu, drained and
  cut into cubes
1 small onion, chopped
3 garlic cloves, crushed
1 fresh red chilli, finely chopped, or
  ½ teaspoon chilli powder
4 celery sticks, thinly sliced
1 bunch spring onions, cut into
  5 cm (2 inch) lengths
175 g (6 oz) Chinese leaves, shredded
2–3 tablespoons soy sauce
salt and pepper
To garnish:
2 eggs, beaten
½ cucumber, cut into short, thin strips

Bring a large saucepan of water to the boil. Add the noodles, cover the pan and immediately remove it from the heat. Leave to stand for 6 minutes. Drain thoroughly.

Heat 2 tablespoons of the oil in a wok or deep, heavy frying pan. Add the tofu and stir-fry over a moderate heat for 2–3 minutes, taking care not to break the pieces up. Lift the tofu out carefully, drain on kitchen paper and keep warm.

Add 1 tablespoon of oil to the wok and heat until hot but not smoking. Add the onion, garlic and chilli and stir-fry for 2 minutes. Add the celery, spring onions and Chinese leaves and stir-fry for a further 1 minute. Add the noodles and soy sauce and season with salt and pepper to taste.

Toss all the ingredients together over a high heat until they are thoroughly heated through. Return the tofu to the wok and carefully stir into the other ingredients.

Heat the remaining oil in a heavy frying pan. Pour in the beaten eggs and make an omelette. Slide the omelette on to a board and cut it into strips. Transfer the mee goreng to a warm bowl and garnish with the omelette and cucumber.

Serves 4

far left: chap-chee
above: mee goreng

Mee Krob

250 g (8 oz) thread egg noodles

3 tablespoons groundnut or corn oil

1 large onion, chopped

2 garlic cloves, crushed

175 g (6 oz) boned, skinned chicken breast, sliced thinly

175 g (6 oz) pork fillet, sliced thinly

125 g (4 oz) green beans, trimmed and sliced in half diagonally

125 g (4 oz) peeled cooked prawns, thawed and thoroughly dried if frozen

300 g (10 oz) tofu, drained and cubed (optional)

3–4 tablespoons cider or wine vinegar

3–4 tablespoons caster sugar

soy sauce or anchovy essence, to taste

oil, for deep-frying

½ teaspoon chilli powder

bean sprouts, to garnish

Bring a large saucepan of water to the boil. Add the egg noodles, cover the pan and immediately remove from the heat. Leave to stand for 6 minutes, then drain and dry the noodles thoroughly.

Heat the oil in a wok or a deep, heavy frying pan. Add the onion and stir-fry over a gentle heat for about 5 minutes until tender. Increase the heat and add the garlic, chicken, pork and green beans and stir-fry for 3–4 minutes. Add the prawns and tofu, if using, and then stir-fry for a further 2–3 minutes.

Gradually stir in the vinegar, sugar, soy sauce or anchovy essence to taste – the sauce should be both sweet and salty in flavour. Remove the pan from the heat. Turn the mixture into a bowl and set it aside.

Heat the oil for deep-frying until hot but not smoking. Add one-quarter of the noodles and fry until crisp and lightly brown. Remove with a slotted spoon and drain on kitchen paper while frying the rest.

Set one-quarter of the fried noodles aside for a garnish. Return about half of the mee krob mixture to the wok with half of the remaining noodles and half of the chilli powder, and toss gently to combine the ingredients and heat them through, taking care not to break the noodles.

Transfer the mixture to a warm serving platter, cover and keep hot while frying the remaining mee krob, noodles and chilli powder in the same way. When the platter is full, garnish with the reserved fried noodles and the bean sprouts. Serve at once.

Serves 6

---

above: mee krob
right: Thai fried noodles with prawns

Thai fried Noodles with Prawns

This tasty snack is enjoyed by Thai children when they return home from school. It can be made with any leftover meat, bacon or ham instead of prawns.

250 g (8 oz) packet egg vermicelli
2 tablespoons vegetable oil
125 g (4 oz) radishes, thinly sliced
4 tablespoons lemon juice
1 tablespoon caster sugar
2 teaspoons anchovy extract
¼–½ teaspoon chilli powder
125–175 g (4–6 oz) peeled cooked
   prawns, drained and thoroughly
   dried if frozen
dill sprigs, to garnish

Cook the vermicelli in a large pan of boiling salted water, according to packet instructions, until just tender.

Heat a wok until hot. Add the oil and heat over a moderate heat until hot. Add the radishes, increase the heat to high and stir-fry for 30 seconds. Add the lemon juice, sugar, anchovy extract and chilli powder. Stir-fry for 1–2 minutes, then add the prawns and stir-fry for 30 seconds or until heated through.

Drain the vermicelli and add to the prawn mixture. Toss over a high heat until evenly mixed. Garnish with dill sprigs and serve at once.

Serves 3–4

Szechuan Noodles

375 g (12 oz) thin egg noodles

250 g (8 oz) minced pork

2 tablespoons dark soy sauce

1 tablespoon dry sherry

4 tablespoons groundnut oil or
   vegetable oil

3 garlic cloves, crushed

2.5 cm (1 inch) piece of fresh root
   ginger, peeled and finely chopped

3 spring onions, chopped

1–2 fresh red chillies, deseeded and
   finely chopped

1 tablespoon hot soy bean paste

1 tablespoon peanut butter

175 ml (6 fl oz) chicken stock

salt and pepper

chopped fresh red chilli, to garnish

Bring a large pan of salted water to the boil. Add the thin egg noodles and cook, according to the packet instructions, until tender. Drain well and then divide between 4 individual bowls or one large one.

Put the minced pork in a bowl with the soy sauce, sherry and ½ teaspoon salt. Mix well to coat the pork. Heat the oil in a deep wok or frying pan and add the pork. Stir-fry until lightly browned. Remove and dry on kitchen paper.

Add the garlic, ginger, spring onions and chillies to the wok and stir-fry for 1 minute. Add the hot soy bean paste and peanut butter, and stir over a moderate heat for a few seconds. Add the stock, bring to the boil and simmer for 5 minutes, until thickened. Stir in the pork and cook over a low heat for 1 minute. Ladle the sauce over the noodles and sprinkle with plenty of pepper. Serve garnished with chilli.

Serves 4

Crispy Fried Noodles

500 g (1 lb) egg noodles
1 tablespoon oil
1 garlic clove, sliced
1 piece of fresh root ginger, peeled and finely chopped
3 spring onions, chopped
125 g (4 oz) lean pork, sliced
125 g (4 oz) boned, skinned chicken breast, shredded
3 celery sticks, diagonally sliced

125 g (4 oz) spinach, trimmed and shredded
1 tablespoon soy sauce
1 tablespoon dry sherry
50 g (2 oz) frozen peeled prawns, thawed and dried
salt

Cook the noodles in a large pan of boiling salted water, according to the packet instructions, until just tender – do not overcook. Drain and rinse with cold water.

Heat the oil in a wok or a deep frying pan, add the garlic, ginger and spring onions and stir-fry for 1 minute. Add the pork and chicken and stir-fry for 2 minutes. Add the drained noodles and the remaining ingredients and cook for 3 minutes. Pile onto a warmed serving dish and serve immediately.

Serves 4–6

far left: szechuan noodles
above: crispy fried noodles

Meanwhile, make a flat omelette. Beat together the eggs and salt and pepper to taste. Heat 1½ teaspoons oil in a frying pan and add the eggs. As the edge begins to set, draw the mixture towards the centre and, at the same time, tilt the pan slightly allowing the uncooked egg to run from the centre on to the hot base of the pan to set quickly. Cook until the omelette is brown underneath and soft on top. Slide out of the pan on to a plate or board and roll up tightly; set aside. Blend the sauce ingredients together in a jug.

Cut the chicken and pork into thin strips. Heat a wok until hot. Add the remaining oil and heat over a moderate heat until hot. Add the chicken and pork, increase the heat to high and stir-fry for 2–3 minutes until browned on all sides, then add the prepared vegetables, one at a time, and stir-fry for 1–2 minutes after each addition.

Add the prawns and crab sticks and stir-fry for 2–3 minutes, then add the rice and sauce mixture and toss well. Add salt and pepper to taste, then stir-fry for a further few minutes until the rice is hot.

Slice the omelette into thin strips and arrange on top of the rice mixture. Serve at once, garnished with chopped spring onions.

Serves 4

Ten-variety
Fried Rice

This Thai-style dish has 10 ingredients in addition to the rice. You can vary these according to what you have to hand.

125–175 g (4–6 oz) fresh chicken
   breast fillets, boned and skinned
125–175 g (4–6 oz) fresh pork fillet
2 eggs
2½ tablespoons vegetable oil
1 large red pepper, cored, deseeded
   and chopped
3 tomatoes, skinned and chopped
2 garlic cloves, crushed
3 green chillies, deseeded and
   chopped

250 g (8 oz) cooked peeled prawns,
   thawed if frozen
4 frozen crab sticks, thawed and cut
   into bite-sized pieces
175 g (6 oz) long-grain white rice,
   boiled and drained
salt and pepper
chopped spring onions, to
   garnish
Sauce:
150 ml (¼ pint) chicken stock
2 tablespoons soy sauce
1 tablespoon tomato ketchup
1 tablespoon caster sugar
2 teaspoons lemon juice
2 teaspoons anchovy essence

Wrap the chicken and pork and then place in the freezer for about 1 hour or until just frozen.

above: ten-variety fried rice
right: fried rice; pilau rice

94

Fried Rice

3 tablespoons oil

3 spring onions, chopped

125 g (4 oz) button mushrooms, sliced

3 eggs, beaten

50 g (2 oz) cooked lean ham, diced

50 g (2 oz) frozen, peeled prawns, thawed and dried

175 g (6 oz) long-grain rice, cooked

1 tablespoon sauce

50 g (2 oz) frozen peas, defrosted

Heat the oil in a wok or frying pan, then add the spring onions and mushrooms and stir-fry for 30 seconds. Add the eggs and scramble lightly over a low heat. Transfer to a warmed plate and set aside.

Add the remaining ingredients and stir-fry for 2 minutes. Return the scrambled egg mixture to the pan and cook for 1 minute. Pile onto a warmed serving dish and serve immediately.

Serves 4

Pilau Rice

6 tablespoons oil

5 cm (2 inch) piece cinnamon stick

6 cardamom pods

4 cloves

3 onions, sliced

2 garlic cloves, crushed

2 teaspoons finely chopped fresh root ginger

250 g (8 oz) Basmati rice

600 ml (1 pint) beef stock, preferably homemade

1 teaspoon salt

½ teaspoon saffron threads, soaked in 3 tablespoons boiling water

lime wedges and toasted flaked almonds, to garnish

Heat the oil in a wok, then add the cinnamon, cardamom pods and cloves and stir-fry for a few seconds. Add the onions and stir-fry for 10 minutes until golden. Add the garlic, ginger and rice and stir-fry for 5 minutes, stirring occasionally.

Add the stock and salt, bring to the boil, then simmer, uncovered, for 10 minutes. Stir in the saffron threads and soaking liquid, increase the heat and cook for 2 minutes until the rice is tender and the liquid has been absorbed. Transfer the rice to a warmed serving dish, garnish with wedges of lime and sprinkle with toasted almonds.

Serves 4

Index